PRESENTING with Style

Robert A. Rohm Ph.D.
and
Tony Jeary *Mr. Presentation*

Contributing Authors and Editors:
Guy Harris and Beth McLendon

Cover Design, Layout and Graphics:
Pedro A. Gonzalez

Photos: Robert A. Rohm by Rick Diamond

Published by Personality Insights, Inc.
PO Box 28592 • Atlanta, GA 30358-0592
800.509.DISC • www.personalityinsights.com

ISBN 0-9641080-6-2

Printed in the United States of America
First Edition: June 2006

This book is lovingly dedicated to you

– the shining new stars in business.
May your presentations sparkle as you
shine through the secrets we share.

Table of Contents

Foreword	7
Introduction	9
About the Authors	13
Making the Most of This Book	16
Understanding Human Behavior	19
Chapter 1 Prepare	25
Chapter 2 Plan	43
Chapter 3 Practice	71
Chapter 4 Personalize	81
Chapter 5 Present	95
Chapter 6 Persuade	129
Chapter 7 After the Presentation: Feedback and Follow-up	149
Resource Materials	158

Foreword

Over the years, my travels have taken me far and wide. I have met many wonderful people and have had the opportunity to work with some very gifted individuals. When I heard that two of my good friends, Robert Rohm and Tony Jeary, had teamed up to write a new book, I was very excited! I know these men and the kind of information they both teach.

I first met Robert Rohm back in 1984, when he was in graduate school in Dallas, Texas. He was our Auditorium Class pastor. We had over five hundred people coming to our Sunday morning teaching sessions. Robert would teach the class when I had to be away. He always had a very clear message that was positive and practical for everyone to hear. My wife, Jean ("the Redhead"), would always tell me what a good job Robert did when he taught our class. Over the years I have watched him grow and have been in nationwide seminars where Robert taught. I have seen the powerful impact he has on an audience.

My good friend, Tony Jeary, and I have worked together on several projects over the years. We produced a video series together called, "Inspire Any Audience." I soon learned that Tony has a gift for helping people articulate things they want to communicate, but simply do not know how. I found Tony to be extremely knowledgeable in the area of communication - the field of study to which I have devoted my entire life. Even though Tony knows an incredible amount of information and is an accomplished professional speaker, I have seen him show gentleness and be helpful to many who aspire to be better speakers.

Both Robert and Tony are two of the clearest communicators I have ever heard. Anyone who wants to present information to another person, group or audience, will greatly benefit from this new work they have created together.

Way to go guys! I am proud of both of you!

Zig Ziglar, President
Zig Ziglar Corporation
Dallas, Texas

Introduction

Who should read this book

As Tony Jeary says, "Life is a series of presentations." If you do sales presentations to individuals or small groups — this book is for you. If you do seminar or workshop presentations — this book is for you.

Most people have little or no training in the art of delivering a convincing presentation. With this book, we have combined our experience to help anyone who has the desire to become a better presenter.

Every presentation, from sales to seminars, has common elements. We have collected these common elements into what we call the **6 P's** of *Presenting with Style*: Prepare, Plan, Practice, Personalize, Present, and Persuade. One chapter is dedicated to each "**P**" and we have included one additional chapter containing some items for you to consider after each presentation. You will also find other valuable tips for becoming a better presenter. Each chapter is a collection of tips to help you in that area. Some of the tips refer more specifically to sales, some more specifically to one-on-one presentations, and some more specifically to group presentations. Whatever your specific application, read every tip. You are sure to find something that will help you improve your presentations

Why we wrote this book

Our grandparents grew up in a day when things took time. If they wanted to conduct business with someone before the telephone, cell phone, fax machine, message machine, e-mail and handheld device; they would spend time together talking, dining, and having fun. They spent time developing relationships and working out the details of the business they would conduct. They may have spent a week or more with someone - just to get to know and trust each other and build mutual trust. It may have taken many carefully composed letters and personal exchanges to develop a valuable, long-term business relationship. How interesting it is to talk with an older person about the way business used to be!

Tony and I have both learned to use technology to develop our businesses. In the process, we have been amazed at the many new challenges we face. Now, because of the wonderful technology that gives us several forms of instant communication, time seems different to us than it did to our grandparents. While business relationships are just as valuable today, we tend to see less of one another. We save time by using forms of communication that do not require us to sit together. Both Tony and I recognize that these new ways of communicating demand that we find better, more effective ways to use the time we do spend together.

Early in my working relationship with Tony Jeary as my presentation coach, we both saw the growing importance of a *convincing* presentation to success in business. As people spend less time sharing ideas face to face, convincing presentations become even more critical for effective teamwork. Our society has quickly moved from a personal relationships to a technology-driven environment for many business presentations. Even in a technology-driven world, however, the decisions are still made by humans.

When starting a new business relationship, people want to be convinced. They want to be convinced first, that they can work together; then, that the business they conduct will be successful for both parties. Despite the use of new communication technologies, people still want to know that they are working with someone that they know, like, and trust. Thus, understanding personalities facilitates the personal understanding necessary to create this type of relationship. This understanding gives a clear advantage over the competition even in a high-tech world.

In our high-tech, instant-message world, we are still people working with people! We build relationships with one another. Then we conduct our business or anything else within those relationships. To achieve real success, we must become as skilled at developing relationships as we are at using new technologies. One part of building any type of relationship, business or otherwise, is the ability to understand people. This understanding comes from comprehending personality styles and it equips you to connect more effectively with other people. The other vital part of building strong business relationships is the ability to make presentations that clearly communicate ideas in a way that moves people to action.

Working with people; whether they are clients, business associates, or family members; demands that we learn to communicate more effectively. That is the aim of this book - to help you learn to communicate more effectively.

This book, like many others, grew out of the efforts and cooperation of a team. Tony Jeary, Mr. PresentationTM, has dynamically outlined the components of a convincing presentation. The Personality Insights staff and I have contributed the perspectives of each personality type as it relates to this subject.

As you read this book, I hope that you gain new insights, learn new ideas, and pickup new techniques that will help you *Present With Style.*

Dr. Robert A. Rohm
Founder and President
Personality Insights, Inc.

This book is a vital link between understanding personality styles and developing the ability to make convincing business presentations.

About the Authors

Robert A. Rohm Ph. D.

Dr. Rohm specializes in understanding and teaching about human behavior. He helps people to better understand themselves and others in order to have better relationships and to build more effective teams. Here are his thoughts on this book:

I am often asked where I learned to speak. I suppose my first presentation was at my kindergarten graduation, where I was the Master of Ceremonies. I immediately knew that standing up in front of a crowd in a white sports coat was my idea of having fun!

When I grew up, I DISCovered that I loved speaking to and entertaining an audience because of my "High I" personality style. I also learned how important it is to provide something for each of the four D-I-S-C personality types when I speak. (You will learn about the four personality styles and how to deal with each type in this book.) The "**Ds**" want real substance they can use and apply... RIGHT NOW! The "**Is**" are happy if they are laughing and having fun...a definite part of all my presentations! The "**S**" types want a steady presentation that does not embarrass or offend anyone in the audience. The "**C**" types want truthful information they know they can count on to be accurate. Understanding personality styles makes my presentations more enjoyable to the audience. So, I have more fun, too. I promise you, if you will add this simple technique to your presentations, you will greatly increase your effectiveness in your speaking ability as well as in all of your communication skills.

Regardless of your personality style, speaking takes practice! I have spent years in practice, speaking in every conceivable situation. Oh, yes, I have "flopped" many times, but that is just part of the learning process.

Sometimes you win, sometimes you learn.

This book has secrets that can help you learn to be a better presenter from start to finish. As you become a better presenter, these secrets will help you be a winner, too.

Dr. Rohm founded Personality Insights, Inc. in response to both a growing interest from people about his work with the **DISC** Model of Human Behavior and his commitment to share this vital information with them. He continues to laugh and learn with audiences around the world.

Tony Jeary

Tony specializes in coaching others to give convincing presentations. Here is a personal note from Tony:

I have invested nearly two decades to studying and teaching others about Presentation Mastery™. Through my coaching and training around the globe, I have observed thousands of businesspeople as they delivered messages to many diverse groups of people. I have come to the conclusion that *Life Is a Series of Presentations*, and most of them are designed to convince the audience about something or someone. The ability to convince other people to accept you and your products, services, or ideas is critical to your success in business.

From a motivational speaker selling books and tapes before an audience of 20,000, to an advertising executive pitching a new campaign worth millions of dollars in front of an audience of five, great success is available to those with the ability to present a convincing concept. Even the negotiations for buying the latest new car, home, insurance, or investment requires the ability to convincingly present ideas.

People who really know how to convince others - the ones who get the most sales and the most buy-in - are masters of the details. No issue is forgotten; from choosing the right tool, to learning the organizational structure of the audience, to recognizing the real needs of their audience. Making a convincing presentation is all about a keen sensitivity to both your ideas and your audience. You might be an expert in your field with years of experience, but if your presentation skills are weak, you will not get the business. On the other hand, effective presentations can result in millions of dollars in sales and thousands of dollars worth of goodwill.

For over twenty years, Tony's expertise has been sought after by Fortune 100 companies because of his unique ability to help people succeed in front of any audience. Both his training company and his publications have grown in response to this demand. Increasingly, people ask Tony for help perfecting their ability to persuade others. In this book, he shares the same secrets he teaches his CEO coaching clients — people who travel hundreds or thousands of miles to his *Success Acceleration Studio* and pay handsomely for the opportunity to learn from Mr. Presentation™.

Dr. Rohm, Tony Jeary, and the Personality Insights staff all share this philosophy: "Give value. Do more than is expected." You will find this philosophy woven throughout the pages of this book. We hope to impart that philosophy to you as you read because that is what audiences want (both yours and ours). We all want a little more than we thought we were going to get. We certainly hope that you will feel that we have given you more than you expected every time you use this book. The content, the layout, and the organization were all very carefully put together to minimize your time investment and to maximize your learning.

Making the Most of This Book

This book is designed to help you become a more convincing presenter, by:

Expanding your thinking about the elements of a convincing presentation,

and

Improving your understanding of the people to whom you will be giving presentations.

Like most successful people, you want to locate useful information QUICKLY. You want easy access to the tips you need when you need them. Therefore, we focus on useful facts. We also present examples and stories to give you direction for personal application. Our main goal is not so much to entertain you, but to equip you to win more in business, and in life, than you ever thought possible.

We have selected tips and techniques for each chapter that will work in most business presentation situations. Some presentations will be to one or two people, some will be to 500 or 5000 people. Others will be somewhere in between. Some tips fit smaller groups better, others fit larger groups better. We recommend that you read them all and learn to apply the underlying principles to your situation.

To keep things simple, *we refer to the people listening to your presentation as your **audience** throughout this book*. Depending on your situation, audience could mean a group of people or it could mean one client or prospect.

The different components for each tip

INSTANT MESSAGE

The Instant Message icon denotes a concise key for the concept. Use this summary to quickly find the tip you need. If you are a fast paced individual, you may use this section to scan the book quickly!

QUOTE

The Quote icon denotes an expert's thoughts on this tip. These are quotable quotes, so feel free to use these yourself.

PERSONALITY INSIGHTS

Personality Insights expands your understanding of the concept to include both your natural presentation style and the personality perspectives of your audience. Some ideas are directed toward you as the presenter and your personality style. Some insights highlight the personality types you will find in your audience.

We hope that you are already somewhat familiar with the DISC Model of Human Behavior. If you are not familiar with the DISC model or you would like a quick review, we have included a brief description of the model after this section.

For a more thorough treatment of personality styles, you may want to read one of Dr. Rohm's other books on the topic: *Positive Personality Profiles, You've Got Style* or *Who Do You Think You Are...anyway?*.

N NOTES FOR YOUR BUSINESS

Notes for Your Business gives an example or a key thought for taking the concept into your business. An important key for you to remember: *BEGIN USING THE TIPS RIGHT AWAY.* Practice using them as you make and prepare presentations. Just reading the ideas will not make you a great presenter. You must DO some presentations! It is okay to make mistakes. All great presenters have made mistakes. In fact, you have to make some mistakes to learn how to do it better. Remember that your presentation will always be a work in progress!

Keep making presentations. You do not need to finish this book before you can do it right. You have had success in the past. We are simply giving you these tips so you can become even better!

This book is intended to help you increase your success. Take the tips in this book, one at a time, and try them in your presentations. Use this book as motivation to make more presentations, so that you can learn more as you go! Remember — we learn by doing!

Make the most of this book by personalizing each tip. Use a highlighter or pen to mark key thoughts. Write your own thoughts in the spaces provided. Create your own personal plans for applying each of the 6 **P**'s of *Presenting With Style*.

Now, let's get started!

Understanding Human Behavior

Over twenty-four hundred years ago, keen observers of human nature began to notice predictable patterns of behavior. In time, these observations led to developing the **DISC** Model of Human Behavior to describe these patterns. Understanding these patterns in human behavior will help you improve your understanding of both yourself and others. The charts in this section illustrate the model and serve as a ready reference for you as you read this book.

Each person has an *internal motor* that drives them. This motor is either fast-paced, which makes some people more **OUTGOING**. Or, it is slower-paced, which makes other people more **RESERVED**. The illustration to the right shows this difference graphically. The shading of the arrows from lighter to darker indicates varying intensities of these drives. Close to the midline shows less intensity in the motor activity, therefore light shading. Towards the outer edge shows more intensity in the motor activity, therefore darker shading. You may be extremely **OUTGOING** or extremely **RESERVED**. Or, you may be only moderately **OUTGOING** or moderately **RESERVED**.

OUTGOING

RESERVED

Just as each person has a motor which drives them, everyone also has an *internal compass* that draws them towards either tasks or people. Some people are more **TASK-ORIENTED** - drawn towards tasks. Other people are more **PEOPLE-ORIENTED** - drawn towards people. The illustration to the left shows this difference graphically. The shading of the arrows from lighter to darker indicates varying intensities of this compass drive. Close to the midline shows less intensity in this compass drive, therefore light shading. Towards

T
A
S
K

P
E
O
P
L
E

the outer edge shows more intensity in this compass drive, therefore darker shading. You may be extremely **TASK-ORIENTED** or extremely **PEOPLE-ORIENTED**. Or, you may be only moderately **TASK-ORIENTED** or moderately **PEOPLE-ORIENTED**.

When you put together both the Motor and Compass Activity drawings, you see the Model of Human Behavior illustrated on the next page.

In the diagram on the next page, notice that each **DISC** type has a group of descriptive words that relate to behavioral characteristics of that personality style. These descriptive words show traits or tendencies that describe each type. The main characteristic trait for each type is used as the representative word for that type: Dominant, Inspiring, Supportive, and Cautious.

Notice that people who are:

Outgoing and Task-oriented are...	*DOMINANT*
Outgoing and People-oriented are...	*INSPIRING*
Reserved and People-oriented are...	*SUPPORTIVE*
Reserved and Task-oriented are...	*CAUTIOUS*

Here are some shortcuts you can use in discussing the different types of people:

the *DOMINANT*	type is also known as High **D**
the *INSPIRING*	type is also known as High **I**
the *SUPPORTIVE*	type is also known as High **S**
the *CAUTIOUS*	type is also known as High **C**

This model can help you understand people by describing four main, or primary, personality styles. However, *each individual person will display some of all four personality styles*. This blend of styles within each person is called a style blend. Each person's style blend will have more of some traits and less of others. The types that are strongest in a style blend are called high styles. The types that are less prevalent in a style blend are called low styles.

Outgoing – Task-Oriented	Outgoing – People-Oriented

Dominant
Direct
Demanding
Decisive
Determined
Doer

Percentage of
population:
10–15%

Inspiring
Influencing
Impressionable
Interested in people
Interactive
Impressive

Percentage of
population:
25–30%

D I
C S

Percentage of
population:
20–25%

Percentage of
population:
30–35%

Cautious
Calculating
Competent
Conscientious
Contemplative
Careful

Supportive
Stable
Steady
Sweet
Status Quo
Shy

Reserved – Task-Oriented	Reserved – People-Oriented

Personality Style Blends

Only a very small percentage of people have a personality style blend that is just one high **DISC** type. Most people (about 80%) have two high **DISC** types and two low **DISC** types in their style blend. This means that one **DISC** type may be highest in your style blend, but you probably also have a secondary **DISC** type which is also high. This secondary type supports and influences the predominant type in your style blend. For example:

- A person who has the **I** type highest and **S** as a secondary high type, would be an **I/S** style blend.
- A person who has the **I** type highest and **D** as a secondary high type, would be an **I/D** style blend

While both of the people in the example above are High **I** types, the difference in their secondary traits would make them very different people.

It is less common, but not highly unusual, to have a third high type in a style blend (i.e. **I/SC** or **I/SD**). Approximately 15% of people have three high **DISC** types and one low **DISC** type in their style blend.

This blending of personality styles in each person helps to account for the large variability among people even though there are only four primary types described by this model.

As you looked at the style descriptive words for each type, you may have felt that you could relate to some of the words in several, or even all, of the **DISC** types. The styles where most of the words describe you are probably your high styles. The styles where only one or two words describe you are probably your low styles. That is okay. This is just a reflection of *your* unique style blend.

You can DISCover your unique style blend by completing a personality profile assessment. While it is not necessary to complete an assessment, doing so will help you apply the information in this book more effectively.

To get the most value from this book and to achieve the greatest possible success, we recommend that you complete a custom-prepared DISCovery Report. This report will identify, with great accuracy, how your blend operates in life and in business. It will reveal your natural strengths. It will also highlight the struggles you may face in adapting your style. The report includes specific suggestions for creating an action plan to help you achieve greater success. Learn more about DISCovery Reports at www.discoveryreport.com. Order your DISCovery Report at www.personalityinsights.com.

Personality Combinations

When two people interact, their style blends come together to form a *combination*. This combination is unique to each interaction of people. Adding a third person to the mix forms a different *combination*. The real power in understanding personality information lies in developing the ability to recognize these different combinations and to adapt yourself to each new situation.

If we can understand each other and adapt to each other better, we can enjoy one another more and increase our productivity at the same time. Dr. Rohm's book, *Who Do You Think You Are... anyway?*, explains many of the factors which work for and against harmony in all kinds of relationships. In **Presenting With Style**, we will specifically explore how the combination of your style with the styles in your audience affects your presentation. We will also offer tips on how to make your presentation more convincing based on the styles of the people in your audience.

The great news is that you can learn to relate better to virtually everyone! Your ability to understand and apply personality information to build stronger relationships is known as your Personality Quotient (**PQ**). Learning experts say that people can do little to change their Intelligence Quotient (**IQ**). They say that **IQ** is fairly well fixed at birth. However, unlike your **IQ**, *you can* develop your **PQ**. So, you can have greater success with anyone you meet, whatever their style.

These personality insights can help you increase your effectiveness both in your presentations and in your personal interactions! Use these personality insights to gain a broader perspective on how you present and represent yourself and your business. Your **PQ**, not your **IQ**, qualifies you to effectively interact with others. *Presenting with Style* will help you move through the four steps to raising your **PQ** so that you can become a better presenter.

Four Steps to Raising your PQ

Understand yourself by understanding your personality style.

Understand another person by understanding their personality style.

Adapt your style to have better relationships.

Build better teams where - Together Everyone Achieves More!

As you read this book, you will see other people's actions and reactions from a new perspective. You will begin to understand them better than ever before. You may even begin to think about how they see you, too. As you read each tip and reflect on the **Personality Insights** section, make some action plans and work through them. Have fun exploring how you can apply these concepts in your life and business. These ideas have helped us immeasurably. We are excited to share them with you.

We look forward to hearing about your success!

Prepare

A convincing presentation begins with complete and thorough preparation.
Very few presenters do well when they "wing it." Even great, veteran
presenters like Tony and Dr. Rohm take the time to prepare for *every*
presentation.

1. Start Now - Fix It Later
2. Build Your Arsenal
3. Know the Benefits You're Offering
4. The 7 Subconscious Desires of Your Audience
5. Know Your Audience's REAL Need
6. Find the REAL Buyer
7. What's Their Budget

"Q QUOTE

*" There is no other accomplishment which any person
can have which will so quickly make a career and secure
recognition as the ability to speak."*

– Phillip D. Armour

---

1. Start NOW - Fix it LATER

IM INSTANT
MESSAGE
Procrastination is deadly! Start preparing - NOW!

Many people are expert procrastinators when preparing for a presentation. Are you? Do not wait for the "perfect" time to start. Start now. Get ideas flowing and write them down. Use a yellow pad, flip-chart, whiteboard, computer, or whatever you have at hand. If possible, enlist someone to talk with you so you can brainstorm together. Get the key points out of your mind and written down. This process should not be a big deal. It might only take ten minutes. It should not be a long, painful process, but you must start. Even though it is not difficult or time consuming, many people delay or avoid this step. You can organize and polish your ideas later, but it is tough to organize something that is not yet written down.

If you sit down to create a presentation from nothing at the last minute, you hurt yourself in at least two ways;

1. You give up your thinking time; the time it takes to process and refine your ideas. You need time to think so your ideas can germinate and grow.

2. Your preparation will probably take longer. With three preparation times of 10 to 15 minutes each, you may do in 30 minutes overall what would take 60-90 minutes, or longer, if you tried to do it all at one time.

So, get started! Start as soon as you know that you have the opportunity to give a presentation. Add to your ideas a little at a time, using a 3-D Outline™. (We will explain this idea in Chapter 2 – Plan.) Starting early will help you create a more convincing presentation.

"Q QUOTE
" Proper prior planning prevents a poor performance."
– U.S. Navy saying

PI PERSONALITY
INSIGHTS

The Book of Lists, states that *speaking before a group* is the number one fear of Americans. Fear makes people say "I can't!" Understanding your fears, based on your personality style, will help you recognize, and address, your fears so that you will say "I can!"

Ds and **I**s are OUTGOING, so they may walk into a presentation unprepared and overconfident. Their confidence gives a good show, and it can create the impression of a good presentation. By investing more time in preparation, they can move from good to excellent.

Ss and **C**s are more RESERVED, so they will tend to prepare extensively and still feel that they have not done enough. Their thorough preparation will make the presentation good. They need to beware of their tendency to over-prepare and not rehearse enough.

 Ds fear losing. They will often shy away from a presentation if they think they will be unable to convince someone else. Preparation can build their confidence in their ability to win with the presentation and convince their audience.

 Is fear rejection. They love the spotlight that a presentation gives them, but they tend to procrastinate on preparation. This procrastination can be caused by one of two very different reasons.

1. They may feel the audience will reject them as a person; so, they avoid the presentation in an effort to be certain people still like them. *- or -*

2. They may be so sure that people will like them that they do not feel the need to prepare. They are confident that they can talk their way into - or out of - anything!

Preparation can help **I**s focus on building a great presentation for their audience instead of focusing on their own feelings.

Ss fear uncertainty. Presentations are full of surprises, and they can freeze under the pressure of this fear. Preparation helps **Ss** gain confidence in their ability both to make the presentation and to handle any unforeseen situations that may occur.

Cs fear the illogical. To them, emotions seem illogical. They have to learn to appreciate and connect with other people's feelings. Preparation helps them develop passion for their subject and an appreciation for what the audience might feel. They make more compelling presentations when they are convinced of the validity and correctness of the information.

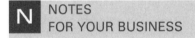

NOTES
FOR YOUR BUSINESS

Do your research. Collect your thoughts. Write them down. Sooner is better than later. Proper preparation will help you address your fears and move past them. Thorough preparation will make your presentation much better.

2. Build Your Arsenal

> **IM** INSTANT
> MESSAGE
>
> *Build quote, anecdote, story, and testimonial files for quick reference. Taking time to build your files repays you with an impressive presentation.*

Quotes, Anecdotes, and Stories

Create a file system to collect and store quotes, anecdotes, and entertaining stories to give life to your presentations. Keep files of magazine clippings, newspaper articles, and notes from books you have read so that you have this information arsenal ready for easy reference. Compile files on your computer by topics, including quotes and their reference, for easy access. File them away mentally, too.

Developing a quote library takes some work, but it is worth it. Become a quote collector. Look for quotes that fit your presentations everywhere you go. You might even carry a small notebook with you to capture quotes when you find them. There are many good places to find quotes:

- The internet *(look for quote collections online)*
- Newspapers and magazines
- Television or movies
- Books of quotations
- Fact or trivia books
- Public personalities/politicians
- An organization's newsletter
- Biographies

When you have a storehouse of quotes and stories to draw from, you can use just the right one for every situation.

Testimonials

It is also a good idea to collect testimonials. Create both a carry-along file and a computer file with copies of your most influential and current testimonial letters. Call or write to satisfied customers and ask them for a testimonial on their letterhead. You can then show or give a copy of the letter to a potential client to validate your claims. It is a good idea to keep a 3-ring binder with the originals of your testimonial letters in protective plastic sleeves. Keep the binder close at hand so you can copy, print, or send high-impact letters to potential clients quickly and easily. Categorize these letters to fit different situations.

Once these past successes are in your mind, in hard copy, and on your computer (or hand-held device), you can access them quickly and easily to pull up quotes from people satisfied with your offering and incorporate them into all of your presentations.

Zig Ziglar, one of the greatest sales and motivational speakers in recent history, is a master at applying this idea. Zig has a wonderful ability to inspire audiences. His mind is like a jukebox (or MP3 player) containing hundreds of anecdotes, quotes, stories, and testimonials for every situation. When the call comes for him to speak, he recalls the appropriate thought, story, or quote from his memory and uses it to clearly communicate just the right idea.

Zig makes it look easy, but do not be fooled. This ability alone does not preclude rehearsal and preparation. No matter how many times he has made a particular presentation, Zig still spends hours in preparation and rehearsal for every talk.

You will deliver more convincing and more powerful presentations if you can include the most appropriate and applicable snippets of information, testimonials, quotes, anecdotes, and stories. To do this, you need to have a way to find them in your mental, paper, and computer files. Once you find them, organize your presentation around them.

Your audience will remember the quotes, anecdotes, and stories. They probably will not remember graphs or data. Do you remember walking away from any presentation with a graph or data slide locked in your mind as the highlight of the day? Probably not! It is the stories that most people remember after the presentation.

"Q QUOTE

" The most potent speeches are often little more than strings of vignettes, loosely linked by an outline."

– Tom Peters

PI PERSONALITY INSIGHTS

Dr. Rohm loves to tell stories! Like any High **I**, he is a natural storyteller. You may also be a natural storyteller. If not, you can learn how to tell engaging and entertaining stories. Stories touch people's hearts and convince them that your ideas have merit. Every personality style tells stories differently. Learn how to tell great stories by listening to someone with a personality style similar to yours who can tell wonderful stories.

N NOTES FOR YOUR BUSINESS

Business is built on relationships and shared through personal stories - both yours and your customers. Whether you are building a relationship, making a one-on-one presentation, speaking to a small group, or making a presentation at a conference; you should compile files of testimonials, quotes, anecdotes and personal stories that relate to your experience, connect with your audience, and tie in to the topic of your presentations.

3. Know The BENEFITS You are Offering

IM INSTANT
MESSAGE
Know the benefits your audience will gain from taking the action you recommend. It is not what you have to offer that counts. It is what you have that the customer needs. Your listener cares what it means to him, not what it means to you.

Think about the wording of this *Instant Message* statement. What is it that makes you and your products, services, or message attractive to your audience? What makes you different from other presenters (your competition)? It may not be what you think.

If you are selling a product or service, determine the main reasons that people buy from you. Consider both logical and emotional reasons. Then, develop your presentation around these reasons. If you are "selling" your message, determine the value that your audience will gain from your message. Answer this question for them: "What can they do or gain by applying your information?" These reasons are the *benefits* to your audience.

Most presenters spend too little time thinking about and presenting the benefits to their audience. Presenters usually emphasize features of their product or service or the logic of their message rather than the benefits. The audience, however, wants to hear how the product, service, or message will benefit them.

Features favor the presenter; benefits favor the listener.

Why do presenters neglect benefits? Perhaps it is because a feature and a benefit are so easily confused. If you think you have a benefit, say it out loud. Then ask yourself, "So what?" If you answer, "Because this is what the product does or has" or "Because it just makes sense to me," then you are thinking about a feature. If it satisfies your audience's need or want, you have found a benefit.

"Q QUOTE
" People want to know the features, but they buy for the benefits."
– Dr. Jeffrey Lant
Thirty Basic Marketing Principles

Different personality styles are interested in *different benefits.*

Ds are driven to accomplish a goal or solve a problem. Find a *feature* and show them how it *benefits* them to **solve their problem.**

Is are drawn to image. Find a *feature* which **enhances their image**, and they will be convinced that it *benefits* them.

Ss are most comfortable with **familiar and well-recommended** *features.* If you can show a *benefit* to their friends, family, or coworkers; they will warm up faster.

Cs require information about special *features.* They may have already identified a desire for these features. If not, **they will research them carefully** after your presentation before becoming convinced of the *benefit* to them. In either case, **they will validate any information you offer before they make a decision.**

N NOTES
FOR YOUR BUSINESS

Some people may already be familiar with the features and benefits of your product, service, or message; but many people will be new to the information you present. Talk with someone you trust, maybe your coach or mentor, and make a list of the features and benefits you have to offer. Ask your audience to tell you what excites them about your offering. Listening to their input will expand your thinking about the benefits you have to offer to people with different personality types. Use this space to record your thoughts on the tip: *Know The BENEFITS You are Offering.*

4. The 7 Subconscious Desires of Your Audience

IM INSTANT MESSAGE

*What people really want is not necessarily what they **say** they want.*

Everyone in your audience will seek to meet some or all of these personal needs:

1. To belong
2. To be respected
3. To be liked
4. To be safe
5. To succeed
6. To find romance
7. To be inspired

These needs are known as the *7 Subconscious Desires of People.* Structure your presentation to address these needs, and you will deliver a convincing presentation.

If you want to satisfy your audience's needs, you must know something about them. What do they need? How can your presentation meet their needs? Too many presenters skip this step. Do not make this mistake! Before you even begin to develop your presentation, seek to understand your audience's needs. The time you invest now will pay big dividends later.

There is a lot of psychology in selling - and in buying. Why do people buy a particular brand or product? Take the desire to belong as an example of one of the seven needs listed above. To meet this need, people might buy because they want to belong to the group of people who already own or use the product or service. To address this need, you should find information about the group of people who already use your product or service. Then reveal this information in your presentation in a way that makes it relatable to your current audience. If they want to belong to the group you referenced, your presentation will lead them to action.

PI PERSONALITY INSIGHTS

If you want to prepare a convincing presentation, make sure that the points you make speak to these 7 subconscious desires. Different personality styles will value some of these desires more than others. Each style will also view the meaning of each desire differently. Taking the desire to belong as an example:

D   High **Ds** want to belong to a group of leaders who make things happen.

I   High **Is** want to belong to a fun group that is exciting to be around.

S   High **Ss** want to belong to a group where relationships are valued and there is low conflict.

C   High **Cs** want to belong to a group that does things the proper way and follows the rules.

Addressing each desire for each personality style is beyond the scope of *Presenting With Style*. For the purposes of this book, we want you to begin the process of recognizing and learning to address these 7 desires in your presentation. You will find a more thorough understanding of each styles' perspective in Dr. Rohm's book, *Who Do You Think You Are...anyway?*

N NOTES FOR YOUR BUSINESS

Learn to answer the 7 subconscious desires of your audience, and you will deliver convincing presentations. You do not have to hit all 7 needs in every presentation, but you do need to learn how to hit enough of them to make an emotional impact on your audience.

5. Know Your Audience's REAL Need

As we said previously, presenting is selling. Here is one truth about selling - you cannot sell anything to anyone; *they* have to decide that they want it. Your job, as a presenter, is to help your audience discover that they need what you are presenting! You want to help them strongly feel their need, and then lead them to the conclusion that what you have to offer will fill that need.

Talk to your audience to find out what they feel is important about your product, service, or message. Put yourself in their shoes. Focus on understanding exactly what they want to achieve and what resources they already have available to achieve it. Target your presentation at filling the gaps in their current resources.

Do not assume that you already know their need. Many presenters fall into this trap. When you think you understand their needs, reconfirm them to be sure you are right. And, your audience may have more than one important need. It is in your best interest to know - and address - all of them. Ask questions, interview people, and do your research. Brainstorm on a flip-chart with the audience, and/or take lots of notes over the phone prior to the presentation to identify their REAL needs.

Remember the standard interview questions: who, what, when, where, how, and why. Use these questions to uncover their needs. Try not to overwhelm them with questions, but develop some simple, open-ended questions that will get the information you need to create a convincing presentation. Use your own words and style to get answers to the following questions:

- Who will be in the audience? or Who will be involved in the decision?
- What do they do?
- What problems are they having?
- What would make it better?
- When do they do what they do?
- Where do they do it?
- How do they do it?
- Why do they do it they way they do it?

- How would they like it to be?
- When would they like the problem solved?

Record their answers to these questions. Remember to capture their *exact* words so that you can quote them in your presentation.

When you present, tell a story that relates to what you have learned about their needs. Dramatize it. Help the audience appreciate how your offer will meet their needs.

Anytime you present (in person, by phone, or by video-conference), your audience is analyzing you. They should leave the presentation feeling that you are on their team, not on their back! If you present to fill their needs, you will be on their team.

"Q QUOTE

" Many speakers fall into a common trap. They approach a subject from a single point of view: theirs. "
– Lani Arredondo

PI PERSONALITY INSIGHTS

You can help your audience DISCover how they need what you are offering! **DISC** helps you see how each person's personality perspective affects what they need and how you can address those needs. It is a great tool for recognizing other people's needs, especially when their needs are different from yours.

Ds need results. They need to know that your product, service, or message will help them solve a problem, get something done, or make a difference.

Is need fun and excitement. They need to know that your product, service or message will be fun for them, make them look good, or be exciting to use.

Ss need safety and security. They need to know that your product, service, or message will create a safe environment, help someone, or enhance peace and harmony. They are not interested in anything that causes conflict or stress.

 Cs need quality answers and value. They need to know that your product, service, or message has been well researched and thought out. They want only the highest quality products, services, or information.

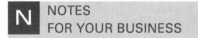 **NOTES FOR YOUR BUSINESS**

Everyone has unfulfilled needs. Show your audience how your offering can help them meet those needs! Dr. Rohm's books, *You've Got Style* and *Who Do You Think You Are...anyway?*, are great resources to help you build even greater understanding in this area.

1

6. Find the REAL Buyer

If possible, find out who makes the buying decision before you make the presentation.

There are typically different kinds of buyers within every organization. *User Buyers* are people who can agree to use your product or buy into your message, but they do not control the money. There are also *Economic Buyers* - people who control the money or make things happen in an organization. User Buyers can often say "no" to your proposal even though they seldom have the authority to say "yes." Courting one while ignoring the other is a recipe for disaster and probably a waste of time. Often, the people in your audience are User Buyers, but the real boss is someone else. Pay attention to User Buyers, but find the Economic Buyer because they can authorize the check being written and get things done.

Your job is to find out who is who - quickly!

To identify the decision-makers, ask questions about organization charts, people's positions, and how their organization works. Tony sometimes gives people a pad of paper and asks them to draw an organizational chart. He also asks where the people in his audience fit into it. Then he can ask questions based on his findings. This exercise can be done on a whiteboard or flip-chart when you are talking with only a handful of people. The audience will usually reveal the real decision-makers and the different agendas of the various players. This kind of information is priceless if you want to persuade your audience to take action on your proposal. It works! Once you understand who makes the decisions, you can build your presentation accordingly.

"Q QUOTE

" The only way to close a sale is to get to the real decision - maker."

– Dr. Jeffrey Lant
Thirty Basic Marketing Principles

PI PERSONALITY INSIGHTS

The real decision-maker may not be the person who talks the loudest or the longest. This behavior often has more to do with personality than with position. The *OUTGOING* personality styles, **Ds** and **Is**, will usually make the most noise. Careful observation will show you whether this person is really the one who makes the decisions.

A friend of ours in the real estate business says that he knows the decision-maker is the one who sits in the front seat with him when they go to look at houses. Take the time to discover the clues that will work for you in your setting and for the kinds of presentations you most often make.

The genius of Tony's organizational chart strategy is that the approach is not offensive. It works, regardless of the other person's personality style, if you are sensitive to your audience's responses. This is a great method to use in a business setting.

N NOTES FOR YOUR BUSINESS

You may be presenting to business partners, co-workers, business teams, or a husband and wife. Some people may be User Buyers and others may be Economic Buyers. Do not assume that you know their roles until you meet with them together. Your goal is to be certain that the key people involved, regardless of their position, buy into what you have to offer.

Deciphering these decision-making roles can sometimes be stressful and time consuming. Friendly words, patient discussion, keen observation, and an open ear will help you work through this process.

7. What's Their Budget?

When possible, pre-qualify your client. Save your time and theirs. If you do not know their budget, your presentation may fail.

Most presentations eventually involve money; money to buy the product or service, money to implement the idea, money to launch a new business.

Ignoring money issues could cause your presentation to fail. If your audience has undisclosed money issues, you will probably fail to convince them to buy in.

If you understand your audience's pocketbook, you can avoid delivering a failed presentation. Slick presentations offering every feature available, but ignoring your audience's budget, are a waste of time; yours and your audience's. Your audience will only take action if the idea you are presenting is within their budget. Audiences look for **ROI** - Return On Investment. Some look for **ROI** at the very beginning, some in the middle, some at the end. But, almost everyone eventually looks at **ROI** before they make a decision.

Present your goods, services, or ideas as a workable solution to a need the audience acknowledges. If possible, cite real life examples of what they can expect and what others have experienced using your product, service, or idea.

People like to get more than they think they deserve. If you create a high perceived value from their investment in your product, service or idea, they will take action!

"Q QUOTE
" Don't think of ways to cut prices. Think of ways to solve your client's problems."
– Dottie Walters

PI PERSONALITY INSIGHTS

Understanding your audience's personality make up may help you interpret how they view their budget.

High **Ds** will usually view a budget as negotiable if the results are good enough.

High **Is** will often ignore a budget.

High **Ss** will depend on a budget for security. They may hide behind a budget so that they do not hurt their relationship with you. Make sure they feel safe, or they will not share their budget with you.

High **Cs** will very carefully formulate a budget and then stick to each detail in it. You will have to show excellent value for the money to get their approval.

N NOTES FOR YOUR BUSINESS

Your audience's budget includes both *time and money*. Respect their perspective on both.

Plan

Sculptors cut, grind, chip, and polish stone to create a final product. The cutting, grinding, chipping, and polishing turns the stone into a sculpture, but they must have a stone to begin.

Your client's needs and your ideas, goals, quotes, and objectives are to a presentation what a stone is to a sculpture - the raw material. You collected these in the Preparation step. When you edit them, rearrange them, take them apart, and piece them together again; you create a more convincing presentation. This work begins in the Planning stage. For a new presentation, you may spend most of your time here. For a presentation you have done before, this step may only involve a few personalizations for your target audience.

1. Know Your Objectives
2. 3-D OutlineTM
3. They Want to See it to Believe it!
4. A Picture is Worth a Thousand Words
5. Quote for Credibility
6. Transitions Bridge the Gaps
7. Planned Spontaneity
8. Curiosity
9. Check for Clarity
10. Dynamic Team Presenting
11. Choosing a Team Leader

"Q QUOTE

" You were born to win, but to be a winner, you must plan to win, prepare to win, and expect to win."

– Zig Ziglar

1. Know Your Objectives

One objective in a convincing presentation is to move people to take action - place an order, join your team, do something to improve their life, or just agree with you on your choice of restaurants. But that is not your only objective. You also want to create a desire for your audience to develop a long-term relationship with you. Think of the future - not just today. If you are making a team presentation, work to make sure everyone on the team has the same objectives for the presentation.

To deliver a convincing presentation, you must keep the objectives of all the involved players in mind. Consider your objectives, the objectives of your employer or partner(s), and the objectives of your co-workers. From the audience's perspective, they have their objectives, the objectives of their employer or partner(s), and their co-workers. Managing all these different objectives takes focus, but it is not as daunting as it may first appear. Once you have asked the preliminary questions in the preparation phase, you are equipped to consider how your proposal impacts all the various parties' interests. If you plan your presentation with everyone's interests in mind, you will better be able to meet all of your presentation objectives.

In general, the main objectives of a convincing presentation are to:

- Provide sufficient, accurate information

- Overcome audience objections

- Create action on or acceptance of your idea

- Lay the foundation to build a lasting relationship or to strengthen an existing one

Common Elements of Convincing Presentations:

1. Background	—	a Brief History
2. Overview	—	the Big Picture
3. Need	—	the Problem to be Solved
4. Idea or Solution	—	the Features and Benefits
5. Proof	—	the Evidence that your Idea will meet their Need
6. Summary	—	a Brief Recap
7. Action	—	the Next Steps

"Q QUOTE

" A problem well-defined is a problem half-solved."

– James M. Bleech
Let's Get Results, Not Excuses!

PI PERSONALITY INSIGHTS

Understanding your audience's personality make up may help you interpret how they view their budget.

Ds are concerned with power. High **Ds** use power to make decisions in order to solve problems. Be ready for a challenge from high **Ds** in your audience. Be prepared to offer bottom-line information.

The **I** issue is people. High **Is** persuade people through interaction. They focus on what is popular with others. Be prepared to provide testimonials or success stories.

The **S** issue is predictability. High **Ss** seek a stable routine to maintain what is acceptable and predictable. Be prepared to show them how to reduce their risk.

Cs are interested in procedure. High **Cs** will proceed according to facts and seek to uphold principles. Be prepared to provide information, answer questions, and to offer third-party sources for validation of your information.

If you want to convince a person to make a decision, plan to speak to the issues that are most important from their perspective.

N NOTES
FOR YOUR BUSINESS

Take the time to personalize your presentation to your expected audience. Consider their personality style(s) as you plan. What kinds of questions or concerns will they likely have? How can you address those concerns during the presentation?

2

2. 3-D Outline™

IM INSTANT
MESSAGE
The Ultimate Presentation Preparation Tool

The 3-D Outline™ is a presentation outline and development tool that Tony developed and has used for many years. He uses it every time he prepares a presentation. After learning about it and how to use it, many presenters consider it to be one of the most valuable tools they use. This 3-D Outline™, helps you to focus on the big picture as you begin sorting your material. You can create 3-D Outlines™ either on a computer or by hand as necessary to fit your needs. This tool lets you make the most of your most valuable commodity - time. We have included a sample 3-D Outline™ below. (Visit www.TonyJeary.com to see the 3-D Outline Builder™ software.)

Notice that the 3-D Outline™ includes all of the vital information you need to organize and create a convincing presentation.

Time	What	Why	How	Who (optional)
15 min	OPEN • Agenda • Purpose	• Get Agreement	• Slides • Discussion	
30 min	BODY • Past • Present	• Paint a picture	• Slides • Lecture	
10 min	CLOSE • Call to • Action	• Encourage Action	• Success story • Ask for order	
55 min TOTAL				

Time : Estimate the amount of time you will have for each segment of your presentation to help you stay within your time limits.

What : Identifies each segment of your presentation. Include only the major points you will be able to cover in the allotted time, with their appropriate sub-points. Use action words - *demonstrate, clarify, show, etc.*

Why: The reason you have chosen the specifics of what you will say.

How: Your method of delivery - lecture, discussion, visual aids, testimonials, etc.

Who: Designates who will present each section of a team presentation.

Develop a logical sequence for the What of your presentation. Remember to organize for the audience's benefit. Meet *your* objectives by meeting *their* needs.

Some Logical Organization Methods

Past to Present Presents material chronologically. This works well when you need to cover historical periods or trace the development of a product, position, or concept.

Priority Presents material in the order of its relative importance.

Advantages and Disadvantages Are presented by showing both the up-side and the down-side of a concept. This method is useful either when presenting controversial material or when informing others before they make a decision.

Pain to Pleasure Takes the audience through an unfortunate, but correctable, situation with a list of possible solutions.

Categorical Requires creating different sections for your material. Organize your material into categories like "Features and Benefits," "Competitive Comparisons," or "Heroes and Villains." The categorical arrangement works well when you have many complex points that need to be presented simply.

"Q QUOTE

" Every speech needs to have a front door, three rooms, and a back door."

— Cavett Robert,
founder of the National Speakers Association

PI PERSONALITY INSIGHTS

A 3-D Outline™, includes each of the favorite questions asked by different personality types. **D**s ask "What?" **I**s ask "Who?" **S**s ask "How?" And **C**s ask "Why?" The genius of this outline is that you will answer all four questions in your design so that you are better prepared to address the needs of any personality style. This outline approach also brings more balance to your presentation.

3. They Want to See It to Believe It!

> *In" Show and Tell," remember that Show comes before Tell! Plan what you want to show using visual aids.*

A study done at the University of Minnesota found that an audience is 43% more likely to be persuaded by a presentation using visual aids than one without them. The study also showed that visual aids, when prepared with the audience in mind, have the added benefit of making the presenter appear more professional, more credible, more interesting, more persuasive, and better prepared. Just remember to keep it simple. Simple truths, demonstrated or spoken with focus and commitment, carry far more weight than complex graphics, charts, and diagrams.

Visual aids (tools) are important to the success of most presentations. If you choose to make a presentation without using visual aids, be sure to have three other things in your favor: a short message, stimulating content, and a very lively delivery style. In most other circumstances, some type of visual aid will improve your presentation.

Six benefits of visual aids:

- Makes it easier for the presenter

- Keeps the audience interested

- Clarifies your message

- Simplifies your presentation

- Gives greater emotional impact

- Guides your presentation

"Q QUOTE
> *" I don't believe that I ever had any doubts whatever concerning the salient points of the dream, for those points are of such a nature that they are pictures, and pictures can be remembered, when they are vivid; much better than one can remember remarks and unconcreted facts. "*
> *– Mark Twain*

PI PERSONALITY
INSIGHTS

Use visual aids to strengthen the areas of your presentation where you naturally struggle. These areas are often tied to your personality style:

D **Ds** may tend to rush through their presentation. Visual aids help them clarify their points so that they do not leave the audience behind. They can also use visual aids to keep other personality styles interested by making the presentation more fun and friendly.

I **Is** may value visual aids most to help them stay focused. They are sure to have a great time, but they need the focus and details that visual aids provide so that they are convincing as well.

S **Ss** may appreciate visual aids that increase the impact of their presentation. Developing interesting and exciting visual aids can help them reduce their nervousness over delivering the presentation.

C **Cs** love clarity. Simple visual aids can improve their presentation. Visual aids can help them introduce humor and simple explanations to provide a very convincing presentation. Remember to keep your visual aids simple and uncomplicated

N NOTES
FOR YOUR BUSINESS

Visual aids can range from writing on a paper flip-chart or whiteboard to PowerPoint™ or Flash™ visuals. Use the *Personality Insights* information to select the right visual aid content for you, your topic, and your audience so that you will make a more convincing presentation. In the next tip, we will look at which type of visual aids to use.

4. A Picture is Worth a Thousand Words

You have decided to use visual aids, and you understand what you want them to contribute to your presentation. After you decide what the visual aids need to show, you are ready to select the type of visual aids needed and design them.

Explore your options. There are many. Computer-generated slide shows (like PowerPoint™ or Flash™), flip-charts, props, and whiteboards are some of the most common types. When you are deciding what type or types to use, consider your audience size and make up. In general, larger audiences call for larger and more formal materials. Create something that can be seen by and have maximum impact on everyone.

> **Note** for large audience set-up: The bottom of your projection screen should be at least 6 feet off the floor. Check to see that everyone in the room has a clear view of the screen.

Computer presentation software

Computer presentation software creates exciting, flexible, visual aids. If you are presenting to a large group, you can build audience anticipation by having something at the front of the room for them to view as they are arriving. Electronic presentations give you plenty of flexibility for building interest. You can display the title page of your presentation, a thought-provoking quote, a cartoon or a company logo on the screen. Creating an electronic "slide show" using changing quotes or other interest builders can add additional variety and interest to your pre-presentation visual aids.

Just remember that slides can make a good presentation great, but they are still just visual aids. They are not the presentation. Tony once sat in on a presentation that used cutting edge technology to create and project their slides. The first few slides were incredibly impressive. But, by the time he sat through 20 slides with the same format, the monotony affected both the appeal and the clarity of the message. Use variety in your slides. Categorize carefully. Be logical. Format them to consistently match your style and message, but do not allow them to become monotonous. Keep the slides simple and uncluttered. Leave plenty of open space on the slide. Avoid the temptation to make them too "slick." Remember - if you lose your audience's attention to the message, you will likely lose your influence with them as well. One good technique for maintaining interest is to intersperse word slides with pictures slides.

Flip-charts

Flip-charts are inexpensive and versatile visual aids. There are no extension cords to trip over, no bulbs to burn out, and no software incompatibilities to crash your presentation. They are low-tech at its finest.

Three basic ways to use flip-charts:

- Prepare them ahead of time – Show everything.
- Reveal information as you go – Show information page by page.
- On the fly - Write notes lightly in pencil on each flip-chart.
  You can see the notes, but your audience cannot see them
  until you write over the pencil with a marker.

Magazine articles

Magazine articles are simple, but valuable tools to use in one-on-one presentations. They are third-party and often can reinforce your point or may even make it for you. This is a tool we suggest you leverage in small presentation settings.

Props

Props are a special kind of visual aid. They create a "memory hook" so that seeing this common item again in the future will remind your audience of your presentation. Props can be as simple as holding up a copy of a book or magazine that you quote from, or storyboards which make great props, too.

Seven considerations for choosing and designing your visual aids

1 Statistics shown visually can be very effective tools of persuasion - if you make them meaningful to your audience. Remember the **3 R's** of presenting statistics:

Reduce Use as few as possible, and only present the most important. Most people will only remember one key statistic in a presentation if they do not write it down.

Round Round them off if possible. Say 4 out of 10 instead of 39%.

Relate Make them relatable. Use a story or comparison to help your audience grasp the significance.

For example, "A PBS documentary about the Civil War reported that 623,000 soldiers died in the war. They followed that number by reporting that more soldiers died in the Civil War than in all other U.S. wars combined." The statistic is helpful. The comparison makes it more memorable.

2 Pie charts are the easiest charts to present, both from your perspective and that of your audience. They are very simple to create, and they are easy for the audience to comprehend.

3 Scale the size of the visual aids to both the room and the size of the audience.

4 Consider both your budget and the costs for developing visual aids.

5 Carefully schedule your preparation time for creating visual aids. Preparation can take longer than you think. Start early in order to make your visual aids the best that they can be.

6 Budget your presentation time to allow your audience enough time to understand your visual aids. Avoid the temptation to go through them quickly.

7 Strategically plan the timing of your visual aids.

> **Note:** You should also change the pace of your presentation by doing part of it without visual aids.

" Visual impressions are like cannon balls; they come with a terrific impact. They imbed themselves. They stick."

– Dale Carnegie

PI PERSONALITY INSIGHTS

Visual aids can help your presentation appeal to a range of personalities. Ask for feedback on your visual aids from someone who is opposite your personality style. Here are some ideas to remember as you apply this tip:

D   **Ds** like bullet points and results-oriented visuals.

I   **Is** like fun, entertaining visuals. Use some humorous pictures to appeal to **Is**. Bullet points work for them, too.

S   **Ss** like visuals that create a good feeling about the information. Pictures of people appeal to **Ss**.

C   **Cs** want facts and data. Make sure everything is spelled properly or they will not trust your presentation.

N NOTES FOR YOUR BUSINESS

Your coach or mentor may already have visual aids available for your most common presentation(s). If you use a whiteboard or flip-chart, practice so that what you do looks sharp.

5. Quote for Credibility

IM INSTANT
MESSAGE
Well-planned quotes increase your credibility and strengthen your message.

Well-planned, meaningful quotes make you and your message more credible. This concept is common wisdom, but it is often overlooked. The concept is known as *Trust Transference*. Tony discusses this topic thoroughly in the "7 Foundational Secrets" section of his great book, *Inspire Any Audience*. By injecting relevant quotes and references, the trust or credibility of the person or book from which you are quoting is transferred to you and your message.

Use quotes to strengthen your message. Your audience will appreciate wisdom that has stood the test of time. When you use quotes, think about both your audience and their personality styles. The most effective quotes relate specifically to the topic at hand, are easy for you to say, and come from a source known by your audience. If you cannot say it clearly or the source is too obscure, the quote may hurt, rather than help, your cause.

"Q QUOTE
" Doing research is like mining for gold: You have to move much dirt to find a nugget."
– Stew Thornley

PI PERSONALITY
INSIGHTS

Quotes bring credibility to you and inspire your audience to believe in you and your message. Different personality styles are convinced in different ways. For example:

Ds give weight to powerful, successful people with direct, results-oriented statements.

Is like to hear quotes from, and to hear stories about, famous and successful people.

Ss get security from the friendly sharing of tried and true wisdom.

 Cs like quotes from research studies, surveys, and experts in the field of study that best fits your message.

N NOTES FOR YOUR BUSINESS

This tip separates great presenters from good ones. Make the effort to listen to other presenters, talk to business leaders, and read books with industry or topic specific information to accumulate applicable quotes. Then, store and categorize them just as you do your stories. Remember the "Build Your Arsenal" tip. This tip brings it together in your presentation.

Be sure to save quotes you get from promotional materials and company web sites so that you can reference them easily. If you have a mentor or coach, they may be able to provide many vital quotes to help you get started!

6. Transitions Bridge The Gaps

| IM | INSTANT MESSAGE |

Transitions join the end of one point to the beginning of the next.

Transitions provide a natural flow between the key points of the presentation. They are instrumental in building and holding audience interest. Here are some simple guidelines for creating good transitions:

- Make them short
- Use attention-getting statements
- Use humor or shock statements (if they are appropriate)
- Use pauses, gestures, body language, and voice changes
- Use statistics that really matter

Some sample transitions:

1 "So, next during our time together today, I plan to show you _____ ."

2 "Now that we have seen, let's take a look at _____ ."

3 "In addition to these accomplishments, we have also been able to _____ ."

Since people can listen four times faster than you can speak, minds wander during even the most gripping of presentations. Use signal phrases like: "What's important here is..." or "This can't be overemphasized." These signal phrases focus your audience's attention on the most important parts of your message.

An effective transition is like a good bridge. It smoothly carries you over the division between your points. Just as a bridge often becomes a landmark on your journey, a transition often summarizes the point you have just made. When you are ready to summarize at the end of your presentation, you can refer to these landmarks to help your audience mentally connnect with your message.

"Q QUOTE
" Not in his goals, but in his transitions is man great."
– Ralph Waldo Emerson

PI PERSONALITY
INSIGHTS

Transitions are good landmarks with different purposes for each **DISC** type.

Ds should use transitions to make sure that they have not rushed through their point too fast and that their audience is still with them.

Is will need to use transitions to check their time and to make sure that they stay focused.

Ss may need transitions to receive encouraging feedback, like a smile or a deep breath. They may also use transitions to provide a powerful place in their presentation.

Cs can use transitions as checkpoints for the emotional, or personal, impact they are having on the audience.

N NOTES
FOR YOUR BUSINESS

As you listen to other presenters, notice the transitions that they use. The way the speaker makes transitions can give you ideas about the kinds of transitions that help you stay with the speaker, that you enjoy hearing, and that you want to use. Effective transitions make the difference between a presentation that draws people in and one that loses them. You must plan to create effective transitions. They are not going to "just happen."

7. Planned Spontaneity

Having complete mastery of your material gives you three clear advantages as a presenter:

1 Credibility with your audience,

2 The confidence to ad lib when appropriate, and

3 The ability to answer questions with authority.

Your audience should know - not by what you tell them explicitly, but by what you show them in your confidence - that you have lots of information on the topic.

Ideally, you should know about five to ten times as much information as you will have time to present. This "information cushion" will give you a huge boost of confidence. With that much information at your disposal, an audience member would find it difficult to stump you with an unexpected question or objection. You will gain great freedom when you have that type of confidence. Spontaneity flows when you plan and prepare thoroughly.

In your planning, develop a ready supply of "come backs" to use when something goes wrong. Develop a clever one-liner to use when the microphone quits, the projector light burns out, or you forget what you were about to say. It sounds original to your audience. It does not matter that you have used it a thousand times before.

Jim Carey spent many hours of his childhood practicing goofy faces in front of a mirror. Now he can, at the drop of a hat, make a fortune by making millions of people laugh. Even though his expressions are practiced, his emotions are fresh. We get to enjoy them again and again, but they did not happen accidentally. He planned them and practiced them purposely and intensely.

"Q QUOTE

" It takes three weeks to prepare a good impromptu
speech. "

— Mark Twain

PI PERSONALITY
INSIGHTS

Spontaneity means different things to different personality types.
Ds and **I**s tend to think that spontaneity means talking "off the top of
your head." **S**s and **C**s think that spontaneity means saying something
in your presentation that was not in your notes. We encourage you to
put planning into your spontaneity, and spontaneity into your planning. If
you are making a team presentation, make sure to plan your spontaneity
so that your team members can anticipate where you are going with it.
You do not want to surprise them!

N NOTES
FOR YOUR BUSINESS

Read books and listen to audios of other speakers on your topic. This
ongoing preparation will build your spontaneity by building your knowledge.
As your knowledge grows, so will the depth of your presentation. Your
ability to add spontaneous examples to your presentation will also grow.
As you gain experience, remember the times when you used a great
"come back" so that you can use it again as planned spontaneity. Plan
spontaneity so you can maintain your sense of humor and adjust to
unforeseen circumstances.

8. Curiosity

Plan your presentation to drop bits of information and open-ended questions as seeds of curiosity at the beginning. Leaving ideas partially open and unfinished keeps your audience interested and involved until the end. This technique is an extremely powerful tool. Here is one example of how to apply this tip early in your presentation - promise a payoff of some kind at the end of the presentation. You could drop a question and promise to reward anyone who can answer it by the end of the presentation. You can call it a bribe if you wish. However, when your audience is listening, even if only to collect the payoff, they are still engaged!

Johnny Carson was a master at using curiosity. He would start a joke, but not finish it. He would then tell a couple of more jokes, and finally come back with the punch-line for the unfinished one. This delivery style created an open loop that kept his audience glued to their seats. Use curiosity to your advantage. Plan how to incorporate it during your presentation.

When you apply this tip, always remember to close the loop by the end of the presentation. If you forget to close the loop, the audience will remember that you did not live up to an implied commitment.

PI | PERSONALITY INSIGHTS

Different personality types can be curious about different things.

D **Ds** will be curious about results and actions.

I **Is** will be curious about the end of stories, tales of excitement, and the punch-lines for jokes.

S **Ss** will be curious about the impact on people and relationships.

C **Cs** will be curious about consistency and logic.

If someone asks a question that you are not ready to answer, use it as an opportunity to build curiosity. Just say: "I'm so glad you asked _____ . I talk about that when we get close to the end of the presentation. May I answer it then?"

N | NOTES FOR YOUR BUSINESS

Withhold some information for curiosity and suspense. Do not tell everything you know all at once. Tell them enough to catch their interest, but not so much that you bore them. Make them curious so that they will focus on what you have to say.

9. Check For Clarity

INSTANT
MESSAGE
There is power in being crystal clear. Make sure that you are.

Write out the objectives you established earlier, and test them against the agenda (3-D Outline™) and the presentation you have developed. Confirm that there is alignment between the overall structure, objectives, and message of your presentation and the needs of your audience.

At a minimum, you should answer these questions in your clarity check:

- What action do you want them to take?
- How can you overcome any objections they will likely have?
- How strong is the case you can make?
- What will your audience respond to best: statistics, humor, emphasis on value, or a combination of these?

Clarify your objectives. Make sure your presentation addresses the questions above.

Now test what you plan to say with the following five questions.

Five Simple Questions to Help You Be Clear

1 If you had only 180 seconds to speak to this audience, what would you absolutely have to say to get your message across?

2 What will set you apart from anyone else they will hear?

3 Why will they remember you, your product, your services, or your request?

4 If your audience had to describe what you said, what would you want them to say?

5 If a newspaper headline was written about your presentation, how would you want it to read?

Testing your message this way will clarify it in your mind. It will help you to ensure that your objectives match your audience's objectives. When you and your audience have the same objectives, your presentation will be more convincing.

"Q QUOTE
" Before you worry about the road to get your results, figure out what you want those results to be."
– Lilly Walters

PI PERSONALITY INSIGHTS

Clear, written objectives do different things for different personality types.

D Written objectives help High **Ds** to focus on their audience and to fill in details that will make their presentation stronger.

I High **Is** can use written objectives to keep their presentation focused on their subject.

S High **Ss** will find that written objectives make them more comfortable with their presentation because they have a predictable plan to follow.

C High **Cs** benefit from written objectives because they enjoy organization. The objectives will help them stay focused on the big picture and avoid getting lost in the details.

N NOTES FOR YOUR BUSINESS

Developing clear, written objectives makes your presentation much more convincing. A clear presentation begins with clear objectives. Be sure to develop your objectives with your intended audience in mind. They will be excited to hear what you have to share!

10. Dynamic Team Presenting

IM INSTANT MESSAGE

Keep your team together. Synergize, don't Separate

Team presentations can have great impact, if you plan and present correctly.

Before the Presentation

- Each team member should have a clear vision of the goal.
- Review written objectives with all team members.
- Build an outline/agenda to hit the target and to focus on the objectives. When possible, do this step as a team.
- Rehearse as a team.
- Plan to dress in a similar style. In general, do not mix jeans and business suits.
- Plan team member to team member transition points and methods.
- Create a written outline of the connection between team members and the sections they present so that it will be clear to everyone when you present.
- Think ahead of time about how each team member should be introduced. Use information of interest to your audience. Your comments should build their credibility by sharing the expertise they contribute to the team presentation.
- Greet attendees as a team.

During the Presentation

- Pay attention to each other's presentations. Keep your eyes on the presenter. Remain silent unless you are asked to contribute.
- Keep in mind the time limits for each presenter. Plan signals to adjust your timing based on the audience.

> " There are plenty of teams in every sport that have great players and never win titles. Most of the time, those players aren't willing to sacrifice for the greater good of the team. The funny thing is, in the end, their unwillingness to sacrifice only makes individual goals more difficult to achieve. One thing I believe to the fullest is that if you think and achieve as a team, the individual accolades will take care of themselves. Talent wins games, but teamwork and intelligence win championships. "
>
> – Michael Jordan
> NBA Basketball Star

PI   PERSONALITY
     INSIGHTS

Team presentations really prove the statement **T**ogether **E**veryone **A**chieves **M**ore! When you draw on the expertise of each personality style in your team, the synergy is exciting. You accomplish something together that no one alone could have done as well. Use this chart to maximize your team's effectiveness.

Provides:	ADVENTURE	
Brings:	DETERMINATION	
Uses:	CREATIVITY	
Stresses:	INNOVATION	

Provides:	IMAGINATION	
Brings:	INSPIRATION	
Uses:	EXPRESSION	
Stresses:	INTERACTION	

Together
Everyone
Achieves
More!

Provides:	ANALYSIS	
Brings:	LOGIC	
Uses:	OBJECTIVITY	
Stresses:	CONSISTENCY	

Provides:	STABILITY	
Brings:	HARMONY	
Uses:	COMPATIBILITY	
Stresses:	SECURITY	

N NOTES
FOR YOUR BUSINESS

Making presentations as a team is common in many business settings.

Your mentor, coach, or team leader can help you understand your part of any team presentation in which you participate. You may facilitate this discussion by asking questions about transitions and the part you will play.

If you are the lead presenter, remember to let each team member contribute the full benefit of their strength.

11. Choosing a Team Leader

Presentation teams should have a leader. Anything in nature with more than one head is a freak!

If your presentation involves a team of two or more people, it is important that you choose a lead presenter. The lead presenter should be a person that relates well to the intended audience and can keep the team focused on creating and delivering a quality presentation. Select a team leader to keep things organized and moving.

The Role of a Team Leader is to:

1　Make clear assignments to each team member to avoid confusion. Confusion creates inactivity.

2　Match individual skills with areas of expertise.

3　Plan who will open the presentation, who will handle each section, and who will conclude and summarize.

4　Hold team members accountable to regularly communicate their progress. For people who work in different locations, e-mail or fax will probably be the easiest way to do this, but everyone should agree on whatever method you choose.

5　Arrange for one or more practice sessions to check: content, flow, transitions, and consistency of terms.

6　Insist that the rehearsal is an actual run-through of the presentation. It is not just a chance for team members to say "What I plan to cover is...."

7　Discuss style of dress and make sure all members agree. In other words, do not mix jeans and business suits.

8　Wrap up the Question and Answer session during the presentation.

"Q QUOTE
" If we are just the same, one of us is unnecessary!"
– Ruth Bell Graham

PI PERSONALITY INSIGHTS

Because High **Ds** are naturally good at driving for results, you might consider asking a person with some High **D** traits to be the lead presenter. The leader does not have to be predominately High **D** - maybe they have the **D** style as one of their strong secondary traits. Whatever their style blend, the team leader should recognize and rely on the personality strengths each team member will contribute to the group. Use the points below (taken from the chart in the previous tip) as a guide to help you in this area.

D   **Ds** provide adventure. They are good at setting the goal and providing drive and energy to the presentation.

I   **Is** provide imagination, fun, excitement, and enthusiasm.

S   **Ss** provide stability. They help the audience feel comfortable and build trust.

C   **Cs** provide analysis. They are good at finding and presenting validated information.

N NOTES FOR YOUR BUSINESS

Many opportunities exist for group presentations. Encourage your team to sharpen their presentation skills. When you have an opportunity to be a team leader, review the *Role of a Team Leader* section on the previous page.

Practice

You have probably heard the statement, "Practice makes perfect!" Now is the time! Take every opportunity you are given to present and learn from every opportunity. You will be amazed at your improvement! Remember - "Anything in life worth doing at all is worth doing *poorly*...until you learn to do it *well*!"

All great presenters practice their presentations. Tony practices. Dr. Rohm practices. Zig Ziglar practices. Practicing your presentation will help you iron out the rough spots, find and correct areas that are unclear, and build your confidence.

1 Practice Pays Big Dividends

2 Visualize Success

3 It's Not So Much What You Say...

4 Listen to a Coach

 QUOTE

" There are always three speeches, for every one you actually gave. The one you practiced, the one you gave, and the one you wish you gave. "

– Dale Carnegie

1. Practice Pays Big Dividends

IM INSTANT
MESSAGE
*Good speakers are not born that way. They may be born with a **desire** to speak, but **everyone** needs to practice, practice, practice to be their best.*

Many people skip rehearsing; do not be one of them. We say, "*Walk through it - don't just talk through it.*" If you can, it is preferable, by far, to rehearse in the actual room where you will deliver the presentation. If you have the option of being on your home turf and being able to rehearse there, take it. If that is not possible, re-create the actual room set-up, as best you can, so you can experience moving around in the setting you will face during your presentation.

During practice, use a tape or digital recorder to record your presentation. Listen to the recording to check your enthusiasm and voice modulation. Listen one time to get the general feeling of the presentation. Then listen again to *really* hear what you said and how you said it. You might even listen to the recording as you drive as one way to mentally walk through the presentation.

Video recording is even better than audio recording. With a video recording, you can critique your presentation with a team to give you an even better feel for the audience's perspective. Carefully observe your tonality and body language. It is best if you can have someone else watch and discuss the recording with you. Most people are too critical of themselves to objectively assess themselves. Most of us tend to believe someone else's assessment of our strengths (and weaknesses) more than our own. Either way, more insight is better.

"Q QUOTE
" All candidates run on virtually the same platform, so what they actually say is not a factor. What is important is how good they are at saying it."

– Robert J. Ringer

Ds and **I**s might be tempted to skip rehearsing because they do not want to take the time to do a presentation more than once. It may get boring! The urge to skip rehearsing for the **S**s and **C**s might come from their reluctance either to make the presentation or to be critiqued by someone else.

 If **D**s want to improve their presentation, a rehearsal will show them what really works.

If **I**s want to refine a presentation, a rehearsal will help them improve their performance so that they look better.

Practice will help **S**s feel more at ease for the real presentation. They need to resist the urge to be harder on themselves than anyone else would be.

Cs need to rehearse so that they are comfortable with the material and confident in their ability to present the information clearly. Rehearsal also helps them think through possible problems and questions that they might encounter.

N NOTES
FOR YOUR BUSINESS

Your presentation will improve and your influence will grow as you practice, practice, practice! Soon, making a presentation will be as easy as a conversation with a friend. If you have difficulty with certain points; get a friend, mentor, or coach to listen to your presentation and give you tips for improvement.

2. Visualize Success

*Do a mental walk-through of your presentation before
you go on.*

Use your 3-D Outline™ to mentally walk through your presentation
before you begin. Visualize various possible scenarios: a changed set-up,
more or fewer people, different decision-makers in the audience, etc.
When possible, Tony puts a few extra chairs in the back of the room, just
in case. This preparation allows him to visualize extra people coming into
the presentation, and it makes him truly ready.

Think through all of the possible weak spots in your presentation.
Consider how difficult situations might occur. Then visualize how you
would handle these situations successfully.

Anticipate the flow. Can the room be set-up beforehand? Where
will you stand? What will happen at breaks? Will there be breaks? What
will happen after a break? Literally and mentally rehearse. If you are
presenting with other team members, include them in thinking through
your presentation steps as well.

"Q QUOTE
" Begin with the end in mind."
– Stephen R. Covey,
The 7 Habits of Highly Effective People

PI PERSONALITY
INSIGHTS

For the **Ss** and **Cs**, the more **RESERVED** styles, this walk-through
helps them feel more comfortable with the unpredictable part of any
presentation. For the more **OUTGOING Ds** and **Is**, the walk-through
helps them see details they may have overlooked. Whatever your type,
thorough preparation, followed by a mental walk-through, will maximize
your chances of presentation success.

N NOTES
FOR YOUR BUSINESS

Picture what you want to happen, and then fill in the details to
accomplish your objectives.

3. It's Not So Much WHAT You Say...

IM INSTANT
MESSAGE
Over ninety percent of the way we communicate is non-verbal.

Studies show that *ninety-three percent* of the way we communicate in person is non-verbal. *Thirty-eight percent* is tonality and *fifty-five percent* is body language.

Tony finds that many people put too much emphasis on their words and not enough emphasis on their non-verbal messages. While coaching people all over the world, he sees that people often spend eighty to ninety percent of their preparation time on seven percent of the message - building visual aids and deciding what words they are going to say. Then they only spend about ten or twenty percent of their time, if they spend any time at all, thinking about the other ninety-three percent of their message - body language and tonality. If you want to be an excellent presenter, concentrate on the non-verbal messages as well as the words.

Consider everything from where you stand to your mannerisms, facial expressions, voice inflection, speaking pace, accent, and pauses. All of these non-verbal clues greatly influence how your audience perceives you.

Think about your movements.

Movement serves a variety of purposes:
- To visually support your message
- To hold your audience's attention
- To release pent up nervous energy

Make your movements meet these objectives so they will match your message.

Use a conversational tone.

Vary your delivery. Speak faster or louder in some places, and slower or softer in others. Use a variety of tones, pitches and activities to avoid boring your audience. Insert some well-planned pauses. "Non-stop bop" can be just as deadly as "hum-drum drone." Audiences need both high and low points to keep their focus on you and your message.

Notice what your audience is telling you

Pay attention to non-verbal communication from your audience, too. Just because they are not throwing rotten tomatoes does not mean they are accepting what you are saying. Learn to read your audience and change your words, body language, and tone to meet their needs, not yours.

> **"Q QUOTE**
>
> *" Deafness has left me acutely aware of both the duplicity that language is capable of and the many expressions the body cannot hide."*
>
> *- Terry Galloway*
> American Performance Artist, b.1950

PI PERSONALITY INSIGHTS

Your body language is another expression of your personality. You may have strengths as well as struggles here, too. Keep in mind that a strength pushed to an extreme can become a weakness.

D — **Ds** - You come across as confident, energetic, and in control. You may need to learn to include a more gentle, personal tone to vary your presentation - especially if you want to appeal to High **Ss** .

I — **Is** - You project warmth, charisma, and sparkle as you make your presentation. You may need to learn to use a more factual tone to vary your presentation and appeal to High **Cs** .

S — **Ss** - You make your audience feel comfortable, accepted, and open to what you have to say. You may need to learn to project more confidence and speed up your presentation in places to appeal to High **Ds**.

C

Cs - You are often the technical expert. You can gain the attention of your audience through your careful preparation and your logical, detailed presentation. You may need to include some personal stories or fun visuals so that your audience will feel warmth and humor during your presentation. Learn to vary your voice tones. High **Cs** tend to have the most difficulty avoiding monotone presentations. Tonal variety will help you relate to your audience more convincingly - especially the High **Is**.

N NOTES
FOR YOUR BUSINESS

Team presentations can be a very effective way to add variety to your presentation. If you can work with someone who is the opposite of your personality type, you improve the odds of connecting with more people. You can make presentations more effectively as a team, and use each other's strengths to create a well-rounded and convincing presentation.

4. Listen to a Coach

Finding a presentation coach or mentor instead of simply studying to improve on your own is similar to hiring a personal trainer instead of going to a group aerobics class. You receive personalized, customized instruction that helps catapult you beyond your current skill set.

Both individuals and companies hire coaches. Individuals hire coaches for personal benefit. Companies benefit by building better presentation skills within their organizations.

Many companies have hired Tony to help them coach one or more people within their organization. The people Tony coaches then become role models within the company. As a result, other people learn the skills that have been taught/transferred to the coached person and become as good as they are. The person who is coached soon becomes the standard by which all other peers are recognized.

Why would you hire a coach or listen to a mentor?

- When you want to land a high-dollar contract or make a presentation to a new client
- If you have the opportunity to make (or lose) big money for yourself or your organization
- When you will be making a presentation as part of a team and you need to be certain everything runs smoothly
- If one of your team members is an expert on the product or service, but is not an effective presenter
- If you want to improve your presentation effectiveness

Professional coaches and experienced mentors can point out subtle nuances or sometimes glaring mannerisms in your performance that limit your effectiveness. People that are close to you or have known you for a while may have learned to ignore these mannerisms. Or, they may be hesitant to point them out to you for fear of offending you.

One technique you can borrow from professional coaches is watching a videotape of your presentation - with the sound turned off! Without the sound as a distraction, you can focus on body language and gestures as you watch. What you see may startle you!

"Q QUOTE

> " A major benefit of coaching is having someone who helps you see your strengths and weaknesses and use them to accomplish your goals."
>
> – Minneapolis Star-Tribune

PI PERSONALITY INSIGHTS

Your coach should be someone with whom you relate well. Find someone who presents well, and who can help you relate according to your personality style. If you are a High **C**, for example, you may learn by observing a High **I** presenter, but you may relate better with another High **C** who can show you how to make a better presentation within your style.

N NOTES FOR YOUR BUSINESS

Personal coaching is popular right now. Find someone you trust and relate to well. Your coach can help you improve faster than you would if your were on your own. They should be a knowledgeable presenter who is willing to speak the truth to you. Remember to recognize and respect your personality and theirs so that you can use your strengths and theirs. If you are a business leader, you might consider hiring a coach to work with key members of your team.

Personalize

You have Prepared, Planned, and Practiced. Now you can focus your attention on the people who will receive your presentation - your audience. They want you to convince them of the value of what you have to say, but they will receive it on their terms. So, you need to understand not only what you have to offer, but also how they will best understand, accept, and act on your presentation. Use these tips to help you find ways to personalize your presentation to your audience.

1 Learn about the People in Your Audience
2 Get to Know Your Audience
3 Make a Personal Connection
4 Get Agreement on Your Agenda

 QUOTE
" People who concentrate on giving good service always get more personal satisfaction as well as better business. How can we give better service? One way is by trying to see ourselves as others do. "

– Patricia Fripp, CSP, CPAE

1. Learn About the People in Your Audience

To make a convincing presentation to a group of people, you must relate to *each individual* in the group - especially the ones who are able to take action. Once you convince the "movers and shakers," your message will turn into action. If your presentation is to an individual or a small group (two or three people), remember that their decisions will likely be influenced by people who are not present at the time. Your primary focus should be on the personalities of the people in the room with you, but you still need to consider what information will be related to people with influence who are not present.

You can easily ask questions that show your personal concern for people in your audience. Your concern for them shows that you are focused on providing quality service that will benefit them and their organization. When people help you understand their concerns and needs, you can become a powerful resource to help them accomplish their goals.

Understanding your own personality style will help you get to know your audience better. If you understand yourself, you can focus your attention on maximizing your presentation strengths and minimizing the impact of your blind spots.

OUTGOING types, **D**s and **I**s, find it easy to start a conversation with someone new. Their blind spot can be pushing their perspective before learning about the other person's. If you are an OUTGOING type, focus your attention on learning about your audience before you speak.

RESERVED types, **S**s and **C**s, find it easy to listen to other people. Because they are RESERVED, they might not actively engage new people or ask specific questions to help them learn how to better relate to the audience. If you are a RESERVED type, learn to guide the discussion so that you can get the information you need to deliver a dynamite presentation.

The table below gives you some additional specific items you can learn about your audience - and why you need to know each of them. These are important regardless of the personality styles in your audience.

You need to know:	So that:
Age Range	You can reference life experiences you share.
Education Level	You know what type of language is best. The lower the education level, the more concrete your language should be.
Occupation	You can use stories and anecdotes that they can relate to.
Cultural Diversity	You know whether casual or more formal speech and dress are expected.

N NOTES FOR YOUR BUSINESS

Business is built on relationships. Use the chart above to find something that you have in common with an individual or a group. Use this common ground to create the environment for a convincing presentation.

2. Get to Know Your Audience

*Focus on getting to know your audience. Ask **your** questions before the presentation so you will be able to answer **theirs** during the presentation.*

All presentations are a form of selling, even if you are not in a "sales" role. In every presentation, your goal is to convince your audience to "buy" (or buy in to) something. Your audience must first accept you as a person before they will accept the ideas you present. Beginning at the time of your initial contact with your audience; focus on their needs.

Sales trainers know that many sales are lost because the salesperson is so anxious to impress prospects with the product that he ignores their questions and comments. Whether you are selling cars, phones, services, or just your ideas; the same principle is true. Many presentations (sales) are lost because the presenter (salesperson) is so anxious to impress the audience (prospect) with information that he ignores the audience's questions, comments, and concerns. Here are some tips to help you "Get to Know Your Audience."

Notice the environment

A person's environment often says something about them. Be sure to notice the surroundings - the decor, the room set-up, banners or pictures on the walls, etc. Look for information in the environment that will help you personalize your presentation and connect with your audience.

Learn to use the names of people in your audience

If your presentations are usually in a business-to-business sales capacity, get to know the receptionist and the decision-maker's assistants. Master the simple things like checking the correct pronunciation and spelling of unusual last names. If your presentations are usually to groups, show up early and get to know some of the people in your audience before you present.

4

Investigate the organization's and audience member's philosophies, goals, and aspirations

Use the Internet. Ask them to send you their marketing information. Pick up brochures in their reception area. Keep their business cards. Go beyond just getting the information – *study* it. What does it tell you about your audience? What are their commitments to quality and professionalism? To convince them, you have to know them.

Know their organizational chart and decision making structure

In working with organizations, understanding their organizational chart is extremely valuable to understanding their world. Get a copy if you can. If not, ask someone to draw out a rough copy. This tip applies if you work with couples as well as it does if you work with businesses. Learn to identify who makes decisions on what issues.

Do your homework to *understand your audience*. The answers to these six vital questions set the stage for a successful presentation:

Six Vital Preparation Questions

1   Will people who have influence, but are not decision-makers, be in the audience?

2   Can the audience members act/decide immediately?

3   If they can decide immediately, what commitments can they make?

4   What are their "hot buttons?"

5   What do they expect from you? Do they want or need a certain style of presentation or materials to feel comfortable with you?

6   How do the key decision-makers like to have information presented to them - by fax, e-mail, phone, or in person?

"Q QUOTE
" Never overestimate your audience's knowledge base; but never underestimate their intelligence."

– Jan D'Arcy

PI PERSONALITY
INSIGHTS

We have used a **TASK-ORIENTED**, High **D** approach in this section. We focused on the *goal* of a convincing presentation, and we want to help you focus on accomplishing that goal as well. If you are more **PEOPLE-ORIENTED**, you may feel that this section is too direct. You may feel that you naturally get much of this information as you talk with your audience. Our point is this, *intentionally* get the answers to these questions to make sure you prepare properly for the presentation. Do not leave gathering this vital information to chance - make it happen.

N NOTES
FOR YOUR BUSINESS

A web site visit can give you quick access to the big picture of an organization. Be sure to use it!

If you make presentations to individuals, you might look at a web site of their work or hobby interests. If the individual has a partner (or partners), their partner(s) may not be the ultimate decision-maker, but remember to respect their influence. Do your homework about them, too.

If you present to larger groups, look at the web site of the business or organization. Learn to identify which groups and individuals within the organization have influence or decision-making authority.

3. Make A Personal Connection

INSTANT
MESSAGE
Rapport and influence grow from a personal connection with your audience.

People like to do business with people like themselves. Here are some tips to help you connect with your audience.

Connect with your audience *before* your presentation

Whether you are presenting to one person or five-hundred, make the effort to connect with as many people as possible. Find what you have in common. Spend a little time in small talk. Share your common interests and experiences. You and your audience both want to feel that you are friends. If you make a personal connection first, you can relax a little. This connection will help you control any nervousness you may feel. A personal connection also makes your audience more likely to decide in your favor.

Give something to your audience

Provide healthy snacks. Give them a book. Give them something to remember you by. People are more likely to agree with your proposal if they feel grateful to you for a gift. Never underestimate the power of free!

Customize your presentation

Continue gathering intelligence as you talk to your audience before the presentation. Use any new information to adjust your presentation, if necessary, right up to the minute you start presenting. This adjustment helps you to connect with their needs better and to create champions in your audience.

Have a customer or audience member give a short testimonial or comment

By taking the time to talk with people up front, you will be able to refer back to those conversations in your presentation. For example,

"Bob and I were talking earlier about _____ . Bob, would you please say a few words about that?" Using this technique gives you *peer transference* - a transfer of trust and credibility from a peer in the audience to you. If Bob is a trusted and respected peer, his agreement with you will have a positive impact on the rest of your audience.

No one can sell your product or service better than a satisfied customer. If they are present, let them speak. If that is not possible, show a video of them or read a testimonial letter while displaying their picture.

Use personal examples to help the audience identify with you and your idea or product

Data tells, but stories sell. Facts, figures, and logic build credibility, but they do not sell. Telling personal stories puts more of you into the presentation. Tell some stories early in your presentation to connect with the audience. Tell your audience about the similarities between you and them that you discovered during your preparation and discussion times.

Share any potentially negative information up front

Determine any feature(s) of your product, service, or message that could be received negatively by your audience and mention it early. Then overcome the objection with your presentation. This show of honesty builds credibility.

Use your audience's jargon

It is a great rapport builder. People like other people who understand and speak their language.

Make yourself approachable

You need to be good, but not perfect. Being too "slick" breaks the emotional connection between you and your audience. They must be able to relate to you before they can trust you.

Use people's names

Here are two tips to help you remember and use your audience members' names:

1 Create a room layout drawing by drawing circles or squares on paper to represent tables in the room. As meeting attendees are introduced, label the positions with names. Take the drawing to the front of the room when you begin your presentation so you can refer to their names as you speak. This technique works well for audiences of fifty or less.

2 Place tent cards in front of each audience member. Write (or have them write) their names on both sides of the card. With their name on both sides of the card, you can see the name from anywhere in the room. Other audience members can see each other's names, too.

Laugh at yourself when you make mistakes

It is the rare presenter who does not make *some type* of mistake *some time* during a presentation.

Tony was once presenting a workshop to the employees of a large retail book chain. The presentation was going well, and he was right where he wanted to be. Then he inadvertently made a positive comment about their chief internet competitor. Whoops! Rather than gloss over or ignore his slip of tongue, he acknowledged his mistake and laughed with them. Because he honestly dealt with his mistake, he endeared himself to, rather than alienated himself from, the audience. They felt that they could relate to him. And they bought into his message.

> **"Q QUOTE**
> *" Laugh at yourself, but don't ever aim your doubt at yourself. Be bold. When you embark for strange places, don't leave any of yourself safely on shore. Have the nerve to go into unexplored territory."*
>
> *– Alan Alda*

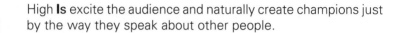

PI PERSONALITY INSIGHTS

Recognize your personality strengths in building rapport.

D High **Ds** love to network. They naturally draw on testimonials. They are comfortable talking with new people.

I High **Is** excite the audience and naturally create champions just by the way they speak about other people.

S High **Ss** befriend people easily and give a sense of calm security to the audience.

C High **Cs** are intensely focused. This intensity can attract the audience to them - especially if they are prepared to share what they know in a friendly manner.

N NOTES FOR YOUR BUSINESS

Good rapport is critical to successful presentations. Use these tips to build rapport with your audience. Especially remember that your audience may not be familiar with your business jargon. Make sure you speak *their* language. (See Tony's book *Life Is a Series of Presentations* for additional ideas on rapport.)

4. Get Agreement on Your Agenda

IM	INSTANT MESSAGE

*Include a place in the very beginning to do a **verbal survey** of the audience to confirm their expectations of the agenda.*

Establish mutual agreement between you and your audience about what you are - and are not - going to cover during your presentation. Audiences like to know what you are going to cover and how it fits their needs.

Set the guidelines in the beginning, and obtain agreement from as many people as possible. Tell them that in order to stay on task, meet your objectives, and finish on time, you need to _____ .
(Fill in the blank with whatever fits your situation.) Here are some specific steps you can take to ensure agreement on your agenda.

Share your agenda to provide a brief overview and to create early agreement

You can show your agenda in several ways. Depending on the size of your audience; you could use a hand-out, post it on a wall, or display it in a computer-generated and projected slide. Whatever medium you choose, be sure that each participant has a clear view of the agenda. You can maximize the probability of audience buy-in and acceptance of your message by providing visual clues about what comes next.

If you are using projected slides, you can post the agenda between each segment of the presentation as a transition slide. Highlight the next item on the agenda each time you show it, so your audience can easily see where you are in the presentation.

Have an opening discussion with your audience

Ask everyone to give you their expectations. If possible, adjust your agenda based on their input. If you make an adjustment, tell the audience that you have done so. This show of flexibility demonstrates both personal confidence and a willingness to adapt to their needs and expectations.

When you are confident in your message, you will feel the freedom to make last minute adjustments to your agenda based on audience input. This flexibility (remember planned spontaneity?) demonstrates that you have full command of your information and are in control of the presentation.

If you do not feel seasoned enough to make adjustments on the spot, you still need to confirm your audience's expectations. Check with them occasionally to see that they agree with the direction of the meeting. When they agree with your direction, they are giving you permission to lead. When they give you permission to lead, they are more likely to follow your lead when it comes to taking action on your proposal. Remember — leading people to action is what persuasion is all about.

If the group is too large to hold an opening discussion, you could try one of Tony's favorite techniques. He gives each audience member a way to have their personal questions answered without disrupting the flow of his presentation. He has them write their questions on a 3x5 card and hand it to him during the Question and Answer portion of his presentation. This way he has a chance to connect with many individuals in the audience.

"Q QUOTE
" Make fair agreements and stick to them."
– Confucious

PI PERSONALITY INSIGHTS

Understanding your style will help you become more comfortable and effective in your presentation.

The more **OUTGOING** personality styles, **Ds** and **Is**, will probably feel most comfortable using an open discussion approach. They can easily adjust their agenda on the spot. They might even find it stimulating and exciting.

On the other hand, the more **RESERVED** personality styles, **Cs** and **Ss**, tend to listen more easily. So, they may feel more comfortable accepting input from the audience.

The **TASK-ORIENTED** styles, **Ds** and **Cs**, need to remember to respect the input from their audience in this kind of discussion. Once they gain the requested input, they should seek to answer the audience's questions.

The **PEOPLE-ORIENTED** styles, **Is** and **Ss**, need to remember to stay focused on their presentation objectives as they adjust for the people in the audience.

N NOTES
FOR YOUR BUSINESS

This tip is about working to match the needs of your audience. You are more convincing when you listen to and address the needs, concerns, hopes, and dreams of your audience.

Present

It's "Show Time!" Put everything you have done to this point into action.

1. Eliminate the Four Audience Tensions
2. Let Me Introduce You!
3. Own the Environment
4. Open Strong
5. Prove You are Ready
6. Champions in the Audience
7. Use Persuasive Words
8. Quote Your Audience
9. Materials to Increase Your Impact
10. Make Your Presentation Fun
11. Enthusiasm
12. Intriguing Pauses
13. Movement and Eye Contact
14. Deal with Integrity

"Q QUOTE

" You may never know what results come of your action, but if you do nothing, there will be no result."

– Mahatma Gandhi

1. Eliminate the Four Audience Tensions

The more comfortable people in the audience feel with each another and their environment, the more open they will be to your message. As the presenter, you should take the lead in making your audience comfortable.

Virtually every audience, however large or small, has four common, natural, and subconscious tensions. Become acquainted with these tensions, and address them immediately in your presentation. By alleviating these tensions, you allow your audience to focus on your message without being distracted.

The four tensions exist between:

1. The audience and the audience

Members of the audience often do not know each other well. Address this tension by:
- Getting the audience on their feet and moving
- Having the audience shake hands and socialize with one another

2. The audience and the presenter

The audience often does not know you yet. Address this tension by:
- Building rapport with the audience
- Establishing and maintaining eye contact
- Smiling

3. The audience and their materials

Audience members are naturally curious about the hand-out materials. When they look through their materials, they stop listening to you. Address this tension by:

- Involving the audience with their materials immediately. Give them an explanation of hand-outs, notebooks, etc. as soon as possible.
- Instructing the audience to immediately write their names on their materials.
- Giving the materials only when participants need them.

4. The audience and their environment

An unfamiliar environment is sure to cause tension. Even when audience members know the room, you should make sure that the seats, temperature, and lighting are comfortable. Address this tension by:

- Being aware of the environment
- Making it as comfortable as possible
- Seeking and acting on feedback concerning comfort issues like seating, room temperature, lighting, sound volume, etc.
- Adding breaks to your agenda, if a comfort issue is beyond your control (hard chairs, poor ventilation, etc.). It is better to have a few extra breaks than to have an uncomfortable audience squirming in their seats.

Just being aware of, and sensitive to, these four tensions will make you a better presenter. Far too few presenters ever give these tensions any thought. Always remember this: people buy from people they like. Most people like other people who show that they care. One key to the success of the Mary Kay Cosmetics company is that its founder, Mary Kay Ash, taught her sales staff to act as though everyone they meet has a sign on them reading, "Make Me Feel Important." By addressing the Four Audience Tensions, you treat your audience like they are important.

"Q QUOTE
" Provision for others is a fundamental responsibility of human life."

– Woodrow Wilson

PI PERSONALITY INSIGHTS

Because these tensions relate to how people feel, **PEOPLE-ORIENTED** people are often more aware of these four tensions than **TASK-ORIENTED** people. **I** and **S** types usually relate well to the audience and quickly resolve these tensions. Becoming aware of and having a plan for dealing with these tensions can help the **D** and **C** types be more effective presenters.

On the other hand, **I** and **S** types may sometimes feel these tensions too intensely because they want everyone to like them and to be comfortable. If the tensions are too intense or too difficult to resolve, the **I** and **S** types may struggle to focus on their presentation. This difficulty focusing can cause them to "freeze-up." **D** and **C** types have an easier time focusing on the task at hand and can usually work through these potentially difficult situations more easily.

N NOTES FOR YOUR BUSINESS

Develop a strategy that you will use, based on your personality style, to help you resolve the *Four Audience Tensions* every time you make a presentation.

2. Let Me Introduce You!

IM INSTANT
MESSAGE
Build your credibility with a powerful introduction.

Your introduction should include, at a minimum, these two things:

1. Something you have in common with your audience, *and*
2. Some points to establish your expertise.

It should rarely take more than sixty seconds. Tell them why you have the right to talk to them. The more relevant the introduction, the higher your credibility. Always be willing to share information on your background and other qualifications. Tell them your areas of expertise. Are you the biggest, smartest, most technologically advanced? Maybe you are the hardest-working? Whatever gives you credibility, tell them.

Even better than introducing yourself, take advantage of *trust transference* by having an audience member introduce you.(*Host Introduction*) If a respected member of the group gives a proper introduction, you start with much more credibility. If you have a sponsor or a champion who brought you in, let that person say a few words about why they invited you. This simple act can have a huge impact on your presentation. Realize that even though your sponsor may be really excited about your presentation, they may not know what to say. It is up to you to help. Offer your sponsor a 3x5 card with your introduction printed on it. You can use either large print bullet points or exact wording depending on *their* presentation skill level.

Your 3 x 5 Card Introduction Bullet Points

- How they know you
- Why you are credible
- 1-3 history points
- Why the audience should listen to you

Even if you have just met them, capitalize on this introduction and your relationship with your sponsor or host. Use their name once or twice during the presentation.

"Q QUOTE

> " Men of genius are admired, men of wealth are envied, men of power are feared; but only men of character are trusted."
>
> – Anonymous

PI PERSONALITY INSIGHTS

Each personality type has different hesitations about someone else introducing them. The bullet points on your *Host Introduction* card will make you more comfortable with what they will say about you. Be sure to make them feel comfortable in accepting it. If you recognize *their* style, you may approach them in one of the following ways:

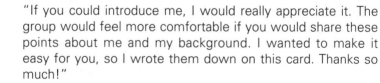

D   "I really respect the leadership you take in this group, and I know how they must listen to you. Would you please introduce me? Here are a few points you can share with them. You will get us off to a great start!"

I   "Your excitement about my presentation is just wonderful! Everyone here recognizes you, so I know it would be great if you would introduce me. Could you include these points in your introduction?"

S   "If you could introduce me, I would really appreciate it. The group would feel more comfortable if you would share these points about me and my background. I wanted to make it easy for you, so I wrote them down on this card. Thanks so much!"

C   "I think that the group would like some information about me before I speak to them. Could you please give my introduction? Here are a few points that you may want to know."

N NOTES FOR YOUR BUSINESS

In a business presentation before a group, a formal introduction is very important. If your presentation is more personal and informal, you might share this card with the person introducing you, and simply say that in formal presentations this is how you are usually introduced. You might then ask them to share the information with your audience so that the audience is more comfortable with you and what you are going to present.

3. Own the Environment

IM INSTANT MESSAGE

Set the environment to work for you. Create an environment where people are free to hear you.

Your attention to the little details, like room set-up, can make, or break, your presentation. You should own your environment and demonstrate that to your audience.

The size of the room should comfortably accommodate the number of people in your audience. If the room is too large for your audience, use only one section of the room.

Take responsibility to make the room work for you. When presenting to a group, plan to arrive early. Anticipate that things will not be set up exactly the way you want them. Set up your equipment and visual aids in advance. Check the lighting, and be sure you know how to control it. If you use a projector, move anything that may block the screen. Make sure that the temperature is comfortable. Sit in chairs in different parts of the room to check the perspective of your audience. Leave enough space around tables or chairs to allow you to walk around and interact with people. In short, check *everything* about the room to be sure that the environment will not cause distractions for your audience. It should enhance your delivery so people will buy in to your message. Recognize the importance of having the environment work for you and not against you. Neutral is not good enough - the room must work *for* you!!

Here is a tip to illustrate how the room can help you. During your pre-presentation set-up, step to the front of the room with notes in hand. Mentally run through the key points and stories. Assign a different object you see in the room to each key point and story. Then, if you lose your train of thought during your presentation, you can look at the object to trigger your memory.

Once you begin your presentation, demonstrate your control over the environment by moving something - a flip-chart stand, the lectern, or your hand-outs - even if it is exactly where you want it to be. You can move it back in a couple of minutes. This simple act demonstrates to the audience that you are in charge of the environment. It is subtle, but the audience will feel your control. If something goes wrong, make a quick adjustment without trying to make your audience think that nothing happened. If you are aware of a problem, at least some of the people in your audience are, too. Let them know you are in control by making a short, preferably humorous, statement about it, fix it, and then move on.

For a one-on-one presentation, you can apply the same principles:

1 Make sure the room is comfortable for the person listening to your presentation, and

2 Move something to demonstrate confidence and control over your environment

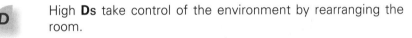

QUOTE *" Things turn out the best for those who make the best of the way things turn out. "*
                                            – John Wooden

PI PERSONALITY
       INSIGHTS

D High **Ds** take control of the environment by rearranging the room.

I High **Is** control the setting by adjusting their feelings to the room so that they can get excited about their presentation.

S High **Ss** usually need more time to get comfortable in a new speaking environment.

C High **Cs** usually check every detail of the set-up so that they feel prepared and in control.

N NOTES
       FOR YOUR BUSINESS

Applying this tip depends on the setting for your presentation. You would apply this differently in someone's home than you would in a hotel meeting room. Understand the concept, and then assess your environment accordingly. Maybe you can move to another room, adjust the lighting, or turn off the television or stereo. Complementing something that you enjoy about the environment your host has created is another way of taking ownership of the environment in a home setting.

4. Open Strong

*You never get a second chance to make a first
impression! Make your first words powerful.*

Your opening statement should capture your audience's attention. Your audience will judge your entire presentation based on the way you begin. Many presentations fail because the presenter takes too long to get to the point. Your main point is not something you build up to - it is how you start. Everything that comes afterword serves to support and reinforce your opening point.

Three Main Goals to Accomplish in Your Opener:

1 Sell your audience on listening to you

2 Introduce your topic and agenda

3 Establish your credibility

Key Ingredients in an Effective Opener:

- Attention-grabbing statement
- Key points which highlight your product, service, or message
- Benefits to your audience
- Words and gestures to communicate your enthusiasm
- Your agenda for the presentation

Open with a hook that will catch the audience's attention - a sixty-second introduction that leaves them wanting more. Some introductions include hooks such as a:

- *Quote* - From a recognized and respected authority.
- *Rhetorical Question* - Involves the audience immediately; a question that creates curiosity is best.
- *Anecdote* - A personal story is very effective since it allows your audience to begin relating to you immediately.

- *Scenario* - "Imagine this..." Make up a scenario that will grab their attention or "Suppose for a moment..."
- *Factual, declarative statement* - Speak it authoritatively and confidently for maximum impact
- *Current event* - A real life situation that is relevant to your presentation

"Q QUOTE

" He can inspire a group only if he himself is filled with confidence and hope of success. "

– Floyd V. Filson

PI PERSONALITY INSIGHTS

Play to your own personality style when you choose an opening statement.

D High **Ds** can be powerful with a declarative statement or quotation.

I High **Is** can be impressive telling a story or describing a situation.

S High **Ss** can be steady with a quotation from a favorite person or a familiar situation.

C High **Cs** can be factual by relating a current event or a relevant quote from an expert on the topic.

N NOTES FOR YOUR BUSINESS

This tip applies both to presenting and to planning. You must plan your opening statement in advance to give it power. Make the opener fit both you and the audience. Remember to create an effective opener for your unique story and your personality style.

5. Prove You Are Ready

If your audience knows that you have thoroughly prepared, you have more credibility with them. Let them know what you have done to prepare for your time together. Take thirty seconds to share some of the specifics of your preparation in a way that will show them how they will benefit from it. Many times your audience has no idea what it takes for you to be effective in making a presentation to them. Weave that information into your presentation without sounding arrogant.

Just one word of caution: while you are proving how qualified and ready you are, do not sabotage your success by saying too much too soon. You must take some time to warm the audience to your subject. Assume that the topic or information you are presenting is new to them. When you are familiar with your message, it is easy to forget how much effort you have put into learning the information. Your comfort with the material could lead you to talk too fast and too much at the beginning. Start with your powerful opening statement, but build in some pauses and slower-paced statements to help your audience "come up to speed." In a one-to-one or small group presentation, you might ask questions that allow them to focus more fully on you and your message. Create a safe environment for your audience to shift gears from what they were doing ten minutes ago to your presentation. When you have their full attention, they will be much more receptive to you and your message.

"Q QUOTE
*" People prefer to do business with VERY confident
individuals. "*

– Dan Kennedy
How to Succeed in Business by Breaking all the Rules

PI PERSONALITY INSIGHTS

Recognizing your style and your tendencies will help you to be more comfortable and balanced in this part of your presentation. Dr. Rohm's book *Who Do You Think You Are...anyway?* offers specific insights to help you in this area. Here are a few tips to help you present in your strengths and stay in control for maximum effectiveness with people.

D   **D**s will naturally prove that they are ready, but they may tend to come on too strong.

I   **I**s will probably tell a great story about their preparation, but they may lose focus and spend too much time here.

S   **S**s will have done extensive preparation, but they may hesitate to show it. They might feel that they are calling attention to themselves instead of realizing that they are sharing information to make their audience more comfortable.

C   **C**s will have extensive validation, but they may overshadow their purpose with too many facts too soon.

N NOTES FOR YOUR BUSINESS

Be ready, at the beginning of your presentation, to subtly let your audience know how much preparation you have given to this presentation. As you make your presentation, you may forget just how hard you worked to learn what you now know. The new person hearing your message for the first time may not catch on immediately. Be confident, but give them a chance to catch up with you.

Remember to share with your audience how you have personalized your presentation for them and how excited you are to be with them.

6. Champions in the Audience

You may identify this person during your pre-presentation research or during your early discussions with the audience. If you can find a champion - however and whenever you do it - do it! Look for someone who will be in your audience and is willing to champion your message. Ask your champion if they would say a few words, explaining how your idea has worked in the past. Have live testimonials planned in advance. Your champions can help reinforce your message and add tremendous credibility to your presentation.

> *" Look for insiders who, for reasons of their own, want you to succeed."*
>
> *– Orvel Ray Wilson,*
> Guerilla Negotiating

Each personality style has its own reasons for becoming a champion.

 High **Ds** want to be powerful champions. They want to talk about results and accomplishments.

 High **Is** will love a chance to be your star. They may want everyone to know that you know them and that they like you.

 High **Ss** will usually shy away from speaking to the group, but they may agree to speak if they believe it will help you.

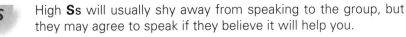 High **Cs** want to provide information. They often like to speak as the expert.

N NOTES
FOR YOUR BUSINESS

Your meeting host or the person who invited you to present may be your champion. Help them to be your champion. Find out, in advance, what they like most about what you will present. Let them know, also in advance, that you will ask them to share.

5

7. Use Persuasive Words

IM INSTANT MESSAGE

The right words matter! Learn to use a persuasive vocabulary.

A Yale University study showed that the words listed below are twelve of the most persuasive words in the English language. Learn to consciously use them in your conversations and presentations.

The Twelve Most Persuasive Words:

YOU	MONEY
SAVE	NEW
RESULTS	EASY
HEALTH	SAFETY
LOVE	DISCOVERY
PROVEN	GUARANTEE

"Q QUOTE

" The most important persuasion tool you have in your entire arsenal is integrity."

– Zig Ziglar

PI PERSONALITY INSIGHTS

We have added the **DISC** personality types most influenced by each word.

YOU	D/I	MONEY	D/C
SAVE	C/D	NEW	I/D
RESULTS	D	EASY	S/I
HEALTH	C/S	SAFETY	S/C
LOVE	I/S	DISCOVERY	D/C
PROVEN	S/C	GUARANTEE	C/S

PI PERSONALITY
INSIGHTS

When you use pre-presentation interview quotes and notes, you are speaking the audience's personality language. Not only are they impressed that you listened to them and their needs, but also by the fact that you are appealing to *their* personality style.

N NOTES
FOR YOUR BUSINESS

Listen to your audience's dreams, feelings, and needs. When you build a presentation around their thoughts and words, they will move to action. Use their words to convince them!

9. Materials to Increase Your Impact

IM INSTANT
MESSAGE
*People remember you by the materials you leave
behind!*

Hand-out materials help people remember your presentation, and they maximize the likelihood that your audience will take action. Make them engaging. Equally important, make the materials theirs. Leave a space on the materials for participants to write in their names.

You can improve the persuasive power of your presentation by using your hand-out materials to establish your leadership. Here is the process:

1 Immediately have each participant write their name on the hand-out materials. This simple act carries a subtle, embedded command that helps to set the tone of your presentation. By asking your audience to write their names on the materials, you start a trend of having them follow what you say.

2 Lead again, early in the presentation, by asking them to respond to a question by raising their hands.

3 Then, ask them to do one more thing - answer a question, write information on the hand-out, complete a short exercise, etc. Have your audience do something that fits a purpose listed in your 3-D Outline™ so that they are following your lead.

This pattern - getting three actions in response to your leadership - creates the precedent of the audience following your lead. This pattern sets the tone for them to follow your recommendation(s) at the end of the presentation.

When preparing your materials, keep in mind:

• What information do you want people to take away from the presentation? Are the materials consistent with your purpose? Do materials already exist to serve this purpose?

- Will the materials be e-mailed in advance, handed out during your presentation, or sent afterwards?

- Will the materials motivate the audience to agree with your proposal? If not, rethink the format and the purpose of the materials.

Other tips and thoughts:

- Reference the materials, but do not read them word for word.

- When possible, include your name and telephone number on each page.

- Keep it short and sweet. If your materials are too long, your audience will not read them.

- People like getting something extra and free. Even a simple, one-page summary of what you said during the presentation is valuable.

- People more easily believe what you say if they also see it in writing.

A tailored hand-out is easy to prepare, and it is a terrific silent partner. It reinforces your message weeks after your presentation.

"Q QUOTE

" While the spoken word can travel faster, you can't take it home in your hand. Only the written word can be absorbed wholly at the convenience of the reader."

– Kingman Brewster,
President of Yale University, Diplomat, 1919-1988

Your materials help you in two important ways:

1. They reflect who you are. They share something regarding your personality. If you are a fun-loving person, they should be visual and fun. If you are very organized, your materials will be, too.

2. Your materials also fill in your personality blind spots. Generally, your blind spot comes from the **DISC** type that is **LOWEST** in your style blend. If you have a:

   LOW D style - your materials can help you make your main points clear and direct.

   LOW I style - use a cartoon to bring a smile to your audience.

   LOW S style - use materials to support your conclusions.

   LOW C style - your charts and graphs can fill in important facts and figures that may be hard for you, and your audience, to remember exactly.

**N | NOTES
FOR YOUR BUSINESS**

Experiment and practice to find the materials that give you the best results. Learn to use both existing materials and to create custom materials as necessary to fit your presentation needs.

10. Make Your Presentation Fun

Create an environment that your audience enjoys. Remember that people learn differently, and include something for each of the three primary learning styles:

- **Visual learners** want to see something. They really connect with visual aids and demonstrations.

- **Auditory learners** will hear what you say. More than the other two learning styles, they will listen to your tone.

- **Kinesthetic learners** want to get their hands on your ideas - literally. Giving them something to do on paper really helps you to communicate with them.

If you teach to their learning style at some point in your presentation, people will *feel* more comfortable.

Create an atmosphere that complements your message so that your audience feels your message. Since atmosphere creates an emotional, rather than a logical, response; know the emotions your audience wants to feel. As a rule, most audience members prefer the atmosphere on the left side of the following chart to the atmosphere on the right. Even audiences with large numbers of professionals, which we usually expect to be more reserved or conservative, have these same expectations.

Enjoyable Atmosphere	Less Enjoyable Atmosphere
Exciting	Serious
Entertaining	Reserved
Engaging	Solitary
Relaxed	Formal
Lively	Slow
Direct	Wordy
Fun	Showy
Inviting	Closed-off
Loud	Quiet

5

Your tones will either engage or turn off your audience. Use the table below to match your tone to what your audience wants to hear.

Tone Audiences Love	Tones Audiences Hate
Conversational	Lecture-oriented
Open	Reserved
Accessible	Aloof
Knowledgeable	Show-off
Confident	Braggart
Entertaining	Dull
Funny	Rude or insulting
Humble	Arrogant
Excited to be there	Perfunctory - I've done this all before

"Q QUOTE

" Never talk to a group. Talk to just one listener at a time. Look directly at him for five seconds...then look at somebody else. It gives the speaker a sense of talking privately."

– Charlie Windhorst

PI PERSONALITY INSIGHTS

Many of the characteristics audiences love in both the presentation and in the presenter are High **I** characteristics. This is understandable when you look at the basic behavioral characteristics of High **Is**. They are good at, and they enjoy, persuading and interacting with people. This is why many of them go to Hollywood to perform!

If your style blend does not have a High **I** part, do not despair. You can develop the skills and learn the techniques that come naturally to them. If you have a High **I** style, notice that some of the undesirable qualities in the chart, such as show-off and braggart, are out-of-control characteristics of High **Is**.

High **Is** need to remember this Secret Tip:

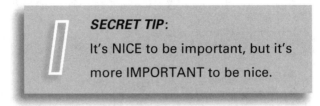

SECRET TIP:

It's NICE to be important, but it's more IMPORTANT to be nice.

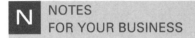

N NOTES
FOR YOUR BUSINESS

What great lists to use as you evaluate and improve your presentations! Take special note of the characteristics you naturally display, and use them to enliven your presentation. If some of these characteristics do not come naturally to you, find a mentor or coach who can help you learn these skills.

11. Enthusiasm

IM INSTANT
MESSAGE

People sense your credibility by your enthusiasm for what you are presenting.

Zig Ziglar says the following about enthusiasm: "If I'm not excited about making a talk, there's not an audience alive that will be excited about hearing that talk. I make every talk as if it's going to be the last talk I will ever make in my life. I can honestly say that when I get off the platform, that audience just got the very best I was capable of doing." No one else will get excited about your product, service, or message unless you do.

People tend to base their beliefs and make buying decisions based on their emotions. They normally justify their decision with logic after they make it. The more passion you express for your product, service, or message, the more you will appeal to their emotions. As you appeal to their emotions, you make yourself more convincing.

"Q QUOTE

" *An audience's biggest turn-on is the speaker's obvious enthusiasm. If you are lukewarm about the issue, forget it!"*

– Tom Peters

PI PERSONALITY
INSIGHTS

More **OUTGOING** people, **D**s and **I**s, usually find it easier to express their enthusiasm. If you have an **OUTGOING** style, let it show! If you have a more **RESERVED** style, **S**s and **C**s, you owe it to your audience to let them see how you feel about your subject. A personal story early in your talk can help you show them how you feel. Remember, it is passion that persuades!

Enthusiasm is contagious! If you hope to get your audience excited and convinced that they need to act on your presentation, you have got to be enthusiastic!

N NOTES
FOR YOUR BUSINESS

It is not easy for **RESERVED** types to show enthusiasm, but it is possible. If you want to be a convincing presenter, learn to show your passion and emotion for your message. You might need to find a mentor or coach to help you in this area. Check your enthusiasm by reviewing audio or video recordings of your presentation. Reviewing recordings helps you see what your audience sees when you present.

12. Intriguing Pauses

Never underestimate the power of a well-placed pause. Pauses add dramatic impact to what you are saying. A pause at the beginning of your presentation will create maximum audience attention.

A pause between the story and the punch line of a joke or the closing point of a story gives your audience a chance to fully grasp the joke or story. The pause adds power to the punch line or the end of the story.

Think about a presenter you have heard who uses pauses well. Did their long pause, lasting one to three seconds, cause you to think that what they were about to say must be very important? The more important the idea, the more important it is for you to pause and let the words sink in before going to the next point.

"Q QUOTE
" The right word may be effective, but no word was ever as effective as a rightly timed pause."
– Mark Twain

PI PERSONALITY
INSIGHTS

An effective pause takes more self-control than speaking does. Often, when a **D** or an **I** is nervous or excited, they will speak too quickly and omit the pause. When an **S** or a **C** is making a presentation, they may feel uncomfortable with silence, since they are the ones who are supposed to be speaking. In either case, slow down and relax. Get comfortable with planned silence.

N NOTES
FOR YOUR BUSINESS

Pauses are all about timing. Listen to great presenters to learn about pauses. Notice how they do it and when. Remember - the more important the idea, the longer the pause.

13. Movement and Eye Contact Matter

Use your movements and eye contact to control the environment. *Move closer to your audience when you want to get their attention regarding a specific point.* This closeness communicates sincerity. When you move around, try to shake hands with people or even sit in a chair in the audience. *Move away from an audience member who is speaking too softly for everyone to hear, and they will naturally speak louder.*

Standing to make a presentation is, in most cases, more persuasive than sitting. When you stand, you and your message are the center of attention. Your gestures are larger and more forceful, your voice is louder, and your overall appearance is more commanding. However, when you present to only one or two people, standing can be too strong. Choose the right posture to create the right environment for your audience size.

Movement and eye contact go hand-in-hand. Always maintain eye contact with your audience for maximum credibility. If you use three to five seconds of eye contact with different people in your audience, you appear more sincere, more convincing, and more confident than the presenter who scans the audience quickly. To keep audience attention, look eye to eye at each person for at least three seconds before looking away.

In a very large group, it may be impossible to look at every person for three seconds. In this case, select people in various parts of the room and make eye contact with them. Ten people around each person you make contact with will have the impression that you are looking at them. By picking a few key people in various parts of the room to connect with, most people in the room will believe that you looked at them personally.

Eye contact is something that you can practice. Go into the room where you will be making the presentation (or another similar room if the designated room is not available) and put a piece of paper on every third or forth chair. Stand at the front of the room and focus on each labeled chair for three to five seconds. You will be amazed at how long three seconds is in this context. You will probably start with only a second or two and assume that it is at least five. This tendency to look away too soon is why we recommend that you practice the art of effective eye contact.

> " I think a speaker loses much when he or she stands there without any gestures, without any emotions, and delivers the presentation – versus the speaker who emotionally gets involved in what he or she is saying. I believe that gestures should definitely be used because God did not create us to be a rock. I want people to look at me and say, ' He's feeling what he's doing.'"
>
> – Nido Quebein

PI PERSONALITY
INSIGHTS

Your personality style really shows in your movements and eye contact.

D   **Ds** tend to be confident in their movement, but they may seem too forceful or abrupt. They are not afraid to make eye contact with their audience. They should remember that the more reserved types may feel that the speaker is staring at them.

I   **Is** tend to be playful and light-hearted, but they may seem like they are clowning around too much if they are not careful. They love to make eye contact. They should remember not to be distracted by the audience response.

S   **Ss** tend to be gentle and open in their movement, but they may seem weak or stiff if they are nervous. They often hesitate to make eye contact with strangers. They give a warm, kind feeling that increases their effectiveness when they do.

C   **Cs** tend to be restricted in their movement, but they can be exquisitely expressive if they lose themselves in their subject. They are guarded in their eye contact, but their intensity really shines when they allow others to see the passion in their eyes.

N NOTES
FOR YOUR BUSINESS

You must get comfortable with your movement and eye contact. Learn to use them to your advantage! Whether you are presenting to one person or speaking to 5,000 people, make your movements and eye contact work together to help you communicate your message more effectively.

5

14. Deal with Integrity

Be yourself. Clearly tell the simple truth, so that your audience knows how you want them to act.

Always deal with integrity. Your audience will be much less likely to buy you, your ideas, or your products if there is any question about your credibility. The more truthful you are, the more effective your presentation will be. This means integrating your words, tone, body language, and visual aids so that they all deliver the same message. Check yourself on this point by reviewing a video of your presentation. If anything looks out of place, fix it!

It is hard to express the importance of integrity any better than Gerry Spence, a courtroom attorney who never lost a case. In his compelling book, *How to Argue and Win Every Time*, he wrote:

"Q QUOTE

" One can stand as the greatest orator the world has known, possess the quickest mind, employ the cleverest psychology, and have mastered all the technical devices of argument, but if one is not credible, one might just as well preach to the pelicans. The lie detector with its operator may take minutes, even hours to complete its analysis of a single sentence. Our minds, as rapidly as the words fall from the speaker's mouth, record split-second conclusions concerning the speaker's credibility. "

– Gerry Spence

Be real, be honest, and you will win business. Keep this 4-S Formula in mind:

STRENGTH + SHORTNESS + SINCERITY + SIMPLICITY = A GREAT PRESENTATION

PI PERSONALITY
INSIGHTS

Look at the 4-S *Formula* from a personality perspective:

D High **Ds** will be attracted by *Strength*.

I High **Is** will enjoy *Shortness*.

S High **Ss** will appreciate *Sincerity*.

C High **Cs** will be energized by *Simplicity*.

A great presentation appeals to all four personality types. As you relax and express yourself, you will exhibit your own strengths and present yourself well. As you deal with integrity relating to your product, service, or idea; you attract your audience to you. This attraction is the first step towards convincing them.

N NOTES
FOR YOUR BUSINESS

Dealing with integrity not only makes a great presentation, but it also makes you a person with whom others will want to do business. People will want to work with you when they feel they can trust you. Make sure that you use Tony's idea of fine tuning your presentation by checking a video of yourself and looking for any integrity gaps in it. (Remember the previous tip of watching the video with the sound off.)

Persuade

You have Prepared, Planned, Practiced, Personalized, and Presented. Now you want to Persuade. You have reached the final point of a convincing presentation. By Persuasion, we mean moving people to action.

■ Humor Opens the Heart
② Get the Audience Involved
③ Speak, Ask, Listen, Summarize
④ Questions and Answers
⑤ Handling Objections
⑥ Close When the Time is Right
⑦ End with a Zoom, Not with a Boom!
⑧ Be Brief, Be Good, Be Gone

 QUOTE

" A good cause is often injured more by ill-timed efforts of its friends than by the arguments of its enemies. Persuasion, perseverance, and patience are the best advocates on questions depending on the will of others."

– Thomas Jefferson

1. Humor Opens the Heart

Get your audience to laugh.

Use humor throughout your presentation to get your point across. It will help relieve tension, and people will like you by association. Audiences almost expect to be bored. They will appreciate you and your message more if you will make the effort to let them have a little bit of fun in the process.

Instead of just starting with a joke to be funny, *create* entertainment that will enhance your talk and make it more memorable. Use variety and drama in your voice and body language. Vary the mood within the presentation. Humor opens people's hearts, so it opens the door for your message. Even if the subject matter is dry, people will rarely complain if you present it in an entertaining and informative way.

"Q QUOTE
" There are three things which are real: God, human folly and laughter.The first two are beyond our comprehension. So we must do what we can with the third."
– John F. Kennedy

PI PERSONALITY INSIGHTS

In promotional material for Dr. Rohm, we love to say "Laugh and learn with Dr. Rohm..." Laughter does different things for different personality types, but it attracts them all to your message.

D **Ds** see your humor as powerful because it shows your ability to control your audience. They will want to listen to you if you are powerful.

I   **Is** evaluate you by your verbal ability, and this is best displayed in your ability to amuse others. They just love to have fun!

S   **Ss** want you to be nice, so a friendly joke will warm them to you.

C   **Cs** appreciate seeing human irony. Do not expect them to roll on the floor in fits of laughter. Rest assured that a smile means they are having fun.

N   NOTES
FOR YOUR BUSINESS

In business, it is okay to have fun! Business is all about relationships. Build strong relationships with people by having some fun in your presentation. Take a moment to think about how you can use your personality style to have fun with your audience.

2. Get the Audience Involved

Get your audience actively involved. Involvement breeds buy-in. Monologues breed boredom. Involving your audience virtually guarantees a more enthusiastic response.

The average adult retains:

- 10% of what he reads
- 20% of what he hears
- 30% of what he sees
- 50% of what he hears and sees
- 70% of what he says
- 90% of what he says and does

In a workshop or seminar presentation, you can use training games to involve small groups. But there are many other ways to involve your audience that do not require facilitating games. Use music, funny videos, skits, role-play, or props. Have them fill-in-the-blank on their hand-out materials. Have them answer questions. Have them work together in small groups. You might simply prepare questions in advance that can help reinforce the major points of your presentation. Be creative. The possibilities are nearly endless.

Be sure to choose an activity that fits your message and your audience. Then give them crystal-clear directions - a confused audience is a frustrated audience. If they become frustrated with your activity, they will be less likely to take action on your recommendations after the presentation.

PI PERSONALITY INSIGHTS

 Ds tend to get bored quickly. Plan some type of activity to keep them from getting too far ahead of you and to keep them engaged.

 Is tend to lose focus if they are not having fun. Plan some type of fun activity to appeal to them.

 Ss like to know what is coming next and how to do things. Make sure you do not surprise them or put them "on-the-spot" with your activities. Create a safe environment for them to participate.

Cs do not generally like activities. They often view them as frivolous. Make sure you can tie your activity to some learning objective so you do not lose credibility with them.

N NOTES FOR YOUR BUSINESS

Activities can enhance both buy-in and learning for your audience. Plan some interactive activity for your presentation so that your audience members really "get" your message.

3. Speak, Ask, Listen, Summarize

IM INSTANT MESSAGE
> *Summarize periodically to be sure that you have clarity and closure as you move from point to point. Summarize at the close to emphasize your main point.*

Summaries are important for five reasons:

1 To give you one more chance to emphasize key points

2 To leave the audience with the main essence of your ideas

3 To make any necessary clarifications

4 To close the Question and Answer session

5 To let the audience know that you are almost finished

Your concluding statements should be positive and upbeat - even if a heated negotiating exchange just occurred. Have your notes in hand so you will not fumble around picking them up after you close. Keep eye contact with your audience and conclude with conviction. After your final sentence in a presentation to a group, keep your eyes on your audience; pause for a couple of seconds; and then leave the front of the room. Their final impression of you will be one of confidence and control.

Closing Phrases to Avoid:

- "Well, that's about it."
- "My time is up."
- "Maybe you could..."
- "If you want to give it a try..."

Good Closing Phrases:

- "In summary..."
- "I'm going to take six minutes to wrap this up..."
- "I've presented the alternatives: I recommend..."
- "In conclusion, the most important point is..."

" Please be good enough to put your conclusions and recommendations on one sheet of paper in the very beginning of your report, so I can even consider reading it."

– Winston Churchill

PI PERSONALITY INSIGHTS

Your summary is vitally important. You probably will have many different personality styles in your audience, so this is a great time to make sure they are attentive and interested in doing what you are going to ask them to do. Find a closing phrase that is comfortable and works for you; then relax and read your audience. You are coming to the finish line!

N NOTES FOR YOUR BUSINESS

Listen to other presenters. How do they close? What words do they use? What body movements? What voice tone?

Your mentor or coach may have a special closing phrase that works well for them. If it feels comfortable, you can use it. If it is uncomfortable for you, it may just be a personality difference. You may be able to make a slight adjustment in delivery to make it work for you. Or, you may need to work on your own closing phrase. Be sure to find one that is comfortable for you so that you are excited and relaxed at this point. Your attention needs to be on your audience and not on yourself.

4. Questions & Answers

The Question and Answer section of your presentation can be an effective way be certain that you have really convinced your audience. Be aware that this section exposes the reaction of one audience member to another. This means that they may confirm the importance of what you have said, or they may discount it. Always place this section before the final close. *The Question and Answer session should not be the last part of your presentation.* It is much too risky to get bogged down in questions *after* you have made your impassioned closing point.

Before you start your presentation, anticipate what some typical questions might be. Then prepare some possible answers for them in advance.

To maintain control of the presentation, give your audience guidelines for their questions. Once you have established the Question & Answer guidelines, a good lead-in would be: "Who has the first question?" or "What questions do you have for me?"

Tips for handling questions:

1 Look at the person asking the question, and let them finish talking before you answer.

2 If the question is very long or complex, ask them to repeat it. This will often clarify the question for you and everyone else. Restate their question so that everyone hears it and to verify that you understood it correctly.

3 It is okay to pause before answering a question. Take a moment to organize your thoughts and to compose your answer.

4 Make sure you actually answer their question.

6

5 Make your answer as concise as possible.

6 If someone asks for something you cannot deliver, say "I understand what you are asking. Here is what I can do…" rather than, "I can't do that."

7 Maintain eye contact with the audience as you answer questions. At a minimum, make contact with the questioner at the start and at the end of your answer.

Stay in control of your emotions when responding to questions. Do not get defensive if the question feels threatening. Maintain objectivity. Treat the person and the question with respect. (Remember: Tact is the art of making a point without making an enemy).

9 Never answer a question by saying that you covered that information in your presentation.

10 Use facts, not just opinions, for at least half of your answers.

11 Ask the person if you have answered their question sufficiently. Simply ask: "Was that helpful?" or "Does that answer your question?"

12 At the end of a long answer, refocus the group's attention by saying something like: "The most important point to remember from this discussion is…"

13 If someone asks a question that you have not anticipated or is off the main topic, here are some helpful responses:

- "Let's get together at the next break to discuss that question."

- "I would prefer handling that question one-on-one after the presentation. It's really beyond the scope of what we are talking about today."

- "I am glad you asked that question, but I really don't have a good answer now. Could you write your question down and hand it to me, so I can get back with you on that question?"

PI PERSONALITY INSIGHTS

Remember that you tend to answer questions the way your personality style would like them answered. Understanding this point and controlling this natural desire can help you better satisfy your questioner. Listen to how they ask the question, and then answer it in the same manner.

Ds often challenge you with a question because they want to know that you really believe what you are saying. Do not be intimidated by the way they ask their questions. Be direct and confident in your answer.

Is love the attention they get from asking questions. If you do not address their questions seriously, they may not get the attention they desire! Be friendly. Make them look good, and they will love you.

Ss may seem nervous or apologetic as they ask their questions. Reassure them that others probably needed to know the answer to their question, too. Let them know that they have helped you by asking it. Answer them gently. Make sure you ask them if your answer was helpful.

Cs usually want clarification or more information when they ask a question. They often need to validate your information with a third party. They would like to know how they can check your information another way or with another source. Be prepared to send them to a web site, book, article, research paper, or expert for validation.

5. Handling Objections

IM INSTANT
MESSAGE

*Addressing common objections IN your presentation
is better than overcoming them AFTER you present.
" NO proofing" your presentation is the best way to
handle objections!*

The best way to handle objections is to solve them beforehand. Carefully step through your presentation and change or get rid of any statement that might create a *no* answer from your audience.

Even after *"NO proofing"* your presentation, it is still very likely that your audience will have an objection or two that you did not anticipate. Here are some ideas to help you handle objections:

Mention a point of agreement before you directly answer the objection

Say something like: "Before I get into that, is it fair to say that we all believe something needs to be done about this situation?" This approach builds a bridge between you and your audience, and it creates some distance from the point of contention.

Admit when you are wrong

Be courageous enough to admit an error. This honesty can actually help your case. Just don't overdo it. A simple and diplomatic acknowledgment of the mistake is all that is required.

Defuse the objection

Find a way to change the words to be more positive, or at least neutral, rather than negative. For example, "That costs too much" can be answered with "Let's talk about the value of my service to your company."

Ask for assistance from team members when you are stumped

Just say something like: "I'm not sure how to best respond to that concern. Could one of you help me out with that one?"

"Q QUOTE
" *You don't need to eliminate all objections, only the critical ones.* "

– Anne Miller
365 Sales Tips for Winning Business

PI PERSONALITY INSIGHTS

How you handle objections relates to your personality style.

 Ds tend to directly address objections. They sometimes look like they are angry with or discounting the person.

Is have a friendly manner that may disarm the objection. They sometimes may appear to be making a joke of the objection or avoiding the real issue.

 Ss usually have great patience that relates well in answering objections. They may tend to avoid the issue in order to shy away from confrontation.

Cs often have information to refute an objection. They may look as if they are personally offended when they are questioned.

You will often get objections that have a personality key to them, as well.

Ds sometimes raise an objection to show that they are in control. This can be especially true in a business situation when they feel that you are competing with them. Acknowledge their importance, and offer them choices when you can.

Is may object on emotional grounds. They may just "feel" that something is not good. You cannot change their feelings, so this is difficult to address. Let them know that you care how they feel about it, and offer to talk with them more after the presentation.

 Ss may offer an objection because they just do not want to change. Pressuring them with facts will only make them more stubborn in their resistance. Acknowledge that change is difficult, and take the time to see that everyone is cared for and comfortable.

 Cs may object for one or both of the following reasons:

1 They naturally tend to have initial negative responses, and

2 They want to validate your information with an objective third party.

Be friendly, and give them the time to talk with someone else. If the situation is right, you might even ask them to report back to the group with their findings.

 NOTES FOR YOUR BUSINESS

A presenter who listens thoughtfully is regarded as charismatic. People will follow their message. Be prepared to answer objections effectively, but always remember to leave on a point of agreement!

6. Close When The Time Is Right

IM INSTANT
MESSAGE
Close when your audience is ready.

Continue to read your audience as you present. If you can tell that they are ready for closure - close. Skip to the end of your presentation when they let you know that they are ready to take action.

If you sense that one section of your presentation is putting them to sleep, quickly move to the next section. Omit any information that is not absolutely vital to the decision you want them to make.

If you are making a sales presentation, why not let your audience sell themselves? Before you close, ask them to list the three best things that they have heard so far. If you should happen to get any negative feedback at this point, STOP! Do not close! Go back, adjust your approach, and present or re-present any information that might change their opinion. If their answer is positive, begin to close.

Once you are ready to close, look for signals that they are ready to make a commitment.

Here are some good signs they are ready for a close:

- A statement such as "That sounds great!" or "I like this..."
- A smile or nod
- Questions about cost, availability, or warranty

"Q QUOTE
" Don't become so enthralled at the sound of your own voice that you miss the buying signals indicating the customer is ready to own."
– Myers Barnes
Closing Strong

PI PERSONALITY
    INSIGHTS

Some closing signs are personality related.

 Ds will most likely make a statement about how great it sounds, or about how they will use it.

 Is will usually tell you how they feel, how they like it, or how they would feel if they used it.

 Ss will most likely give you a smile or nod, maybe saying something reassuring to you, or maybe saying nothing.

 Cs will most likely ask questions about why they would use it in a certain way.

Answer their questions, then roll into the close. You've got it!

**N NOTES
    FOR YOUR BUSINESS**

Your coach or mentor can give you the benefit of their experience by telling you some of the buying signals they have heard. Knowing what you are offering them right now is very important. If you do not understand your offer - your call to action - then neither will your audience. Be careful not to confuse them at this point. Keep the close simple and direct.

Be sure to identify what you are asking them to do. They will not know what to do with your presentation unless you tell them! Clarity is the sign of a good leader.

7. End With a Zoom, Not With a Boom!

> **IM** INSTANT
> MESSAGE
> *Plan a convincing close. Create a simple sentence that summarizes and wraps it all together, and then leads to a decision.*

Your conclusion should grab their attention, stick in their memory, and create a decision in your favor. Audiences want and need an ending that sounds like an ending. Point out the benefits of your proposal. Help them see and feel what will happen for them if they take action. Paint a word picture illustrating the benefits of following your recommendation.

Save enough time for your conclusion so that you do not have to speed through it. It is very important to plan the conclusion. A boring or anti-climactic closing can discount everything you have just said and leave your audience with no need or desire for action. Above all, do not read your conclusion. It is crucial that you maintain eye contact with your audience during the close. Here are some ideas to help energize your closing.

Issue a challenge to the group

This is effective when you are proposing something that requires a change from the status quo. You can ask something like: "Do we/you have what it takes to _____?"

Summarize the major points you made

Your agenda slide would be great here.

Present options

Summarize the possible alternatives. If it is appropriate, emphasize the option that you prefer.

Paint an "imagine this" scenario

Take your audience into the future by describing how things will be different when they have taken the steps you want them to take. Paint an exciting picture to let them feel the success. Talk to them as if they have already taken the action you propose.

Give them facts and figures

Even if you have already quoted statistics, re-emphasize key figures in the closing. Just be sure they are the kind of statistics that create a burning desire for action rather than the kind that create a burning desire for a nap!

Use a quote

Use quotes sparingly. Be certain they completely relate to your presentation and help to establish your credibility. Make sure the person, study, or institution you are quoting is respected by your audience. Short quotes are better than long ones.

End like the beginning

If you painted a word picture to involve them at the beginning, refer back to it, and complete it at the end.

Refer back to your audience champions

Personal references from audience members go a long way to convince others in the audience of your proposal. Imagine the impact of saying that you spoke with the Sales Manager during the break, and that he has already told you he would like to implement your plan. Just be sure you have the Sales Manager's permission to quote him first!

Ask for a decision

Create a solid reason for them to act now. Always close with a call to action. Make it as compelling as possible with a sense of urgency. Many powerful presentations get no action from the audience just because the presenter does not tell them what they should do.

> **"Q QUOTE**
>
> " *The best thing you can do for a prospect is eliminate his fear.* "
>
> – *Harry Beckwith*
> *Selling The Invisible*

If you are making a presentation to a large group, be sure to include as many of these ideas in your close as possible. They each appeal to different personality styles.

High **Ds** will love the challenge and having options. They will require that you ask for a decision. After all, if you do not have the strength to ask, they do not want to do business with you!

High **Is** will love the word picture if it is a good story. They will also respond to your audience champions or a quote, if it is from someone they know and like.

High **Ss** will like for you to go over your main points because it helps them feel comfortable with your ideas. They will respond well to an imaginary scenario if it seems believable to them.

High **Cs** will focus on the key data. They will want to hear the next steps laid out. Include these steps in your imaginary scenario.

N NOTES
FOR YOUR BUSINESS

As you close, emphasize the ideas that will most appeal to the styles present in your audience. If your audience is a large group, you will need to think about something for every personality style. If your audience is only one or two people, just focus on them.

8. Be Brief, Be Good, Be Gone

As Voltaire once said," The secret of being a bore is to tell everything."

Just because you have done your research and uncovered lots of interesting statistics does not mean that you have to share it all. Good presenters do not do a data dump on their audience. They tailor and trim their message to make it meaningful for their particular audience in a way that will influence a positive decision. You do not need to tell your audience everything you know. Tell them only what they need to hear to be persuaded to accept your message.

How many times have you *really* wished a presenter had spoken longer? We would bet, not many! Most presentations could finish more effectively in significantly less time.

"Q QUOTE

" The best speech a salesman can deliver is one that says all that should be, but not all that could be, said."
– S. H. Simmons

PI PERSONALITY
INSIGHTS

A few tips to help each **DISC** type:

D   **D**s keep to their points, but should make sure that their audience keeps up with them.

I   **I**s keep everyone's attention, but should make sure that they stay on time and on track.

S   **S**s keep the audience comfortable, but should make sure that they bring the audience to a decision.

C   **C**s keep a logical sequence, but should make sure to include only the most important facts. Remember - make it fun!

N NOTES
FOR YOUR BUSINESS

What can we say, except, "Keep it simple!"

After the Presentation: Feedback and Follow-up

The presentation may be over, but the relationship continues. What you do after the presentation can mean as much to your success as what you did before and during it.

1 The Secrets of Satisfied Customers
2 Getting Better
3 A Collection of Ideas to Keep in Mind

 QUOTE
" *Feedback is the breakfast of champions.*"
– *Ken Blanchard*

1. The Secrets of Satisfied Customers

IM INSTANT MESSAGE
Become the expert about your audience. Know why someone would listen to you. Get feedback from them!

Do you know why your audience takes action after your presentation? Do you know why some of your customers are now labeled "Previous?" Have you asked?

Use fax, e-mail, and telephone surveys to collect customer feedback. You will receive incredibly valuable information from these surveys. In our experience, many people comment that they are impressed merely by our effort to ask what they thought. You can do similar surveys to find out what people think about your presentation style, image, products, service, etc.

Each year we survey our top 30 to 40 customers by sending them an e-mail or letter with a one-page feedback form that takes about two minutes to complete. Here are some survey tips from our experience:

- Use multiple choice or check boxes rather than essay questions on your survey form.

- If it takes more than two minutes of effort, give them a gift for completing and returning the survey. If you cannot give a gift, make the survey easier to complete.

- Make the survey process clear and easy to understand in your explanation memo.

- Make the process feel simple. Ask them to fax, mail, or e-mail their responses - using the best technology to make it easy and less time consuming for them.

- If you do workshops or seminars, use a feedback form at the end of the workshop or seminar.

To prepare a convincing presentation, you need to know why your audience likes (or dislikes) what you have to offer. You need to know what will cause them to take action after the presentation. Knowing why people have bought from you in the past will help you quickly and efficiently tailor your future presentations to your audience's needs. Remember - the needs of your audience are what it is all about.

"Q QUOTE

" What is the main reason you continue to do business with this company? I just feel comfortable with them. "

– Harry Beck,
Selling the Invisible

PI PERSONALITY INSIGHTS

Write your survey in a friendly manner to engage the people-oriented **Is** and **Ss** who receive it. Careful instructions and a place for individual comments will set the detail-oriented **Cs** at ease. Check boxes are critical if you want the fast-paced **Ds** and **Is** to respond. A personal request for their responses will encourage all styles to respond.

At Personality Insights, we include two questions aimed at identifying the personality style of the respondent. We ask:

1 "Are you more outgoing or more reserved?" - and -

2 "Would you say that you are more task-oriented or more people-oriented?"

These questions help us understand their responses better.

N NOTES FOR YOUR BUSINESS

Survey your newest clients to find the most (and least) effective parts of your presentation. Ask them what you shared that was most (and least) attractive to them. Use these responses to sharpen your presentation. Make every effort to stay current with changes in your business or industry. Keep your examples current. The longer you are in business, the more vital it becomes for you to survey people who are new to the information. It is easy to forget how much you have learned over time. Understanding what people new to your presentation see in it will keep you fresh and interesting.

2. Getting Better

What a great presentation! Take the time to evaluate how you did, and how you can improve next time. When you find something that works with an audience, do you remember it? Immediately make notes about it. Some things will impact multiple audiences. Capture them so that you can use them over again. Learn how to be the best presenter you can be.

Five Common Mistakes that Hurt Your Results

1. Unclear and unspecific objectives
2. Poor preparation
3. Lack of genuine enthusiasm or conviction
4. Poor first impression
5. Weak visual aids and materials

First, use your audience feedback to look for evidence of these problems in your presentation. Then, develop action plans to correct the problems.

Ds and **Is** now must be sure that they follow through well. They may get bored and skip taking notes for the next presentation, but they will not forget to celebrate their success! **Ss** and **Cs** may spend more time taking notes and focusing on follow through, but they need to remember to celebrate their success!

If you are working with a team, depend on your team members who have opposite styles to bring your team balance.

Remember - *Together Everyone Achieves More!*

N NOTES
FOR YOUR BUSINESS

Your mentor or coach is vitally important to your growth and success. Ask them to help you follow through with your audience and be sure to get their input on how to make your presentation even more effective next time!

3. A Collection of Ideas to Keep in Mind

IM	INSTANT MESSAGE

You are always presenting. Stay sharp to gain more business.

- When you make a presentation, consider yourself independently wealthy. If people get the feeling that you need their business or approval, you are dead. People buy because it helps them - not you.

- Keep the first "sale" (or agreement) simple. Get your audience to agree on something small to start the process. Whatever you are "selling" - whether it is goods, services, or ideas - the principle remains the same: once they make the first "buying" decision, they are inclined to "buy" more if you offer it.

- Be easy to do business with. Be accessible. If you present to a group, stay to answer questions after the presentation. If you make sales presentations, make it easy for your clients to contact you. Return phone calls or e-mails promptly.

- Honor your commitments. Develop systems that work for you and your clients. If your client wants periodic progress reports, send them. If the client does not like details, only hit the high points. Adjust the way you work to match the needs of your client.

- If you work in a sales environment, send a written summary of the agreement to your client. Clearly define your expectations and your understanding of their expectations. End with testimonials from others you have helped in similar situations. Emphasize your results.

- Follow-up your presentation with something of value to the audience. Try sending an e-mail summary or a time line of expected actions and outcomes. Keep communication flowing to cement the relationship.

"Q QUOTE

" There is more hunger for love and appreciation in this world than for bread. "

– Mother Teresa of Calcutta

PI PERSONALITY INSIGHTS

Ask someone you know who has a very different personality style from yours if they understand your approach. This may be hard for you because you may feel that they misunderstand you. Remember that many people are just like them, so respect how they can help you communicate more effectively!

N NOTES FOR YOUR BUSINESS

These ideas apply throughout the process - from preparation to presentation. These ideas are more about relationship that showmanship. Your main goal after the presentation is to strengthen the relationship for the long-term.

Remember — people buy from people, not from companies.

Now you can really shine as you continue

Presenting with Style!

The end of this book is just the beginning for you. Take each tip and give it some time to become a part of your presentation style. Expect to learn something from each of your presentations, and be sure to practice by doing! You will find that you learn the most by actually making presentations and expecting great results. The great results will include learning something from each person who listens and interacts with you. You will become more convincing as you gain experience. The success you achieve will keep growing as you do! Keep the excitement growing. It started in your presentation, and it can grow into their dreams and yours. *Now, grow for it!*

Resource Materials

You've Got Style

Dr. Robert A. Rohm

This book is a great guide on understanding yourself and others. It gives all the foundational information about the four personality styles, and it also includes chapters on adapting your style and building better teams. Simple enough to understand, practical enough to apply!

A Tip in the Right Direction - Volume I, II, III

Dr. Robert A. Rohm

Would you be willing to spend two minutes a day investing in your future? This books holds valuable insights that will change your life – AND it only takes a couple of minutes a day to gain this powerful knowledge and real wisdom. Dr. Rohm shares a lifetime of experiences in how to make the most out of life in these easy to read books.

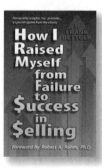

How I Raised Myself from Failure to Success in Selling (Foreword by Dr. Robert A. Rohm)

Frank Bettger

A business classic, *How I Raised Myself from Failure to Success in Selling* is a must read for anyone whose job it is to sell. Whether you are selling houses or mutual funds, advertisements or ideas – or anything else – this book is for you. No matter what you sell, you will be more efficient and profitable – and more valuable to your organization – when you apply the author's keen insights.

To purchase these materials and more go to:

www.personalityinsights.com